Duty to Deter

*American Nuclear Deterrence and
the Just War Doctrine*

Rebeccah L. Heinrichs

Foreword By Keith B. Payne

*Radio,
With hope,
Rebecca Heinrichs*

National Institute Press®

Published by
National Institute Press®
9302 Lee Highway, Suite 750
Fairfax, Virginia 22031

Copyright © 2024 by National Institute Press®

Library of Congress Control Number: 2024943453

Publisher's Cataloging-in-Publication
(Provided by Cassidy Cataloguing Services, Inc.)
Names: Heinrichs, Rebeccah L., author. | Payne, Keith B., writer of foreword.
Title: Duty to deter : American nuclear deterrence and the just war doctrine
               / Rebeccah L. Heinrichs ; foreword by Keith B. Payne.
Description: Fairfax, Virginia : National Institute Press, [2024] | Includes
               bibliographical references and index.
Identifiers: ISBN: 978-0-9855553-5-1 | LCCN: 2024943453
Subjects: LCSH: Deterrence (Strategy) | Nuclear warfare--Prevention. | Nuclear
               weapons--Government policy--United States. | Just war doctrine. |
               Cold War--21st century. | World politics--21st century. | National
               security--United States. | United States--Military policy.
Classification: LCC: JZ5675.H45 2024 | DDC: 327.1/74--dc23

Cover design by Stephanie Koeshall

For my children Charlotte, Howard, Catherine,
Rosemary, and John

Acknowledgments

This book began as an essay, the writing of which revealed both my great enthusiasm for the subject as well as significant knowledge gaps. This combination prompted the pursuit of my doctoral program, culminating in my capstone project, and this book. For that, Keith Payne is due a place of prominence here for his invaluable instruction and for providing the book's tremendous foreword.

My gratitude also goes to Amy Joseph, who facilitated the publishing process. And to the experts who read early drafts and offered recommendations. I am humbled by the commendations offered by remarkably accomplished leaders.

I extend thanks to the Rumsfeld Foundation, the Sarah Scaife Foundation, and Missouri State University's Defense and Strategic Studies scholarship for their generosity.

My colleagues at Hudson Institute make it a vibrant place for experts to offer policymakers principled and pragmatic solutions to advance American security, freedom, and prosperity. This is a legacy of Herman Kahn.

And thanks to Mark Tooley and Marc LiVecche who were the first to encourage me to write about morality and realism with *Providence Magazine*.

I have benefited enormously from the advice and opportunities provided by many. A note of gratitude goes to Elliot Abrams, Marshall Billingslea, Kari Bingen, Matthew Costlow, Henry F. Cooper, Ben Domenech, Eric Edelman, Carrie Filipetti, Mike Gallagher, Rich Goldberg, Lisa Gordon-Hagerty, Brian Hook, Rose Gottemoeller, Jakub Grygiel, John Hyten, Robert Joseph, Robert Karem, Matthew Kroenig, Jon Kyl, H.R. McMaster, Cliff May, Walter R. Mead, Josh Mitchell, Richard Mies, Frank Miller, Tim Morrison, Henry "Trey" Obering III, Mike Pompeo, Matt Pottinger, Charles "Chas" Richard, Brad Roberts, Nadia Schadlow, Gabe Scheinmann, David Trachtenberg,

Josh Trevino, Ryan Tully, Greg Weaver, Chris Yeaw, and Roger Zakheim.

Long before any reflections on U.S. defense policy, let alone nuclear deterrence strategy, I began the intellectual pursuits that would lead to this book as an undergraduate at Ashland University in Ohio. I am especially indebted to my professors at the Ashbrook Center.

Mark Dever of Capitol Hill Baptist Church has faithfully provided years of pastoral care and doctrinal instruction to me, my family, and thousands more in our nation's capital. Joan Dunlop has cheered me on while helping me keep my priorities in order.

My parents, Larry and Jodi Ramey, have been unfailingly supportive and wise counselors. It is a privilege to be their daughter.

Finally, thanks go to my husband, Hanz. He is my most dedicated and trusted advisor, editor, and source of encouragement. It is impossible to convey his extraordinary goodness to me. His gain is mine, and mine his.

Table of Contents

Foreword

There is a seemingly endless supply of books and articles on the subject of nuclear arms and deterrence. Only a fraction of these reflect expertise in the subject areas — which is why the public canon on nuclear deterrence is a decidedly mixed bag. This is particularly true of the episodic public debates about the morality of nuclear deterrence and weapons.

Commentaries on the morality of nuclear deterrence by apparently comparable learned experts often confidently reach wholly contrary conclusions. Where is one to turn when authoritative voices reach contrary conclusions without any apparent uncertainty? The best that one can do is carefully work through the competing texts and logic and try to distinguish between that which is coherent and consistent with available evidence, and that which is activist hype or political agitprop, which may unknowingly be repeated by the unsuspecting novice.

In this text, *Duty to Deter*, Dr. Rebeccah Heinrichs takes on the herculean task of examining, in a transparent and scholarly way, the moral dimensions of nuclear weapons and deterrence policy. Doing so credibly requires a fluent understanding of both moral analysis and nuclear deterrence analysis and policy — a diverse expertise that is exceedingly rare. It is an understatement to note that commentators on this arcane subject, at every level, typically appear to have a superficial familiarity with either moral analysis or deterrence policy, or both — which is one of the reasons the public canon on the subject is so uneven.

To the reader's great benefit, Dr. Heinrichs has spent years focusing on both moral analysis and nuclear deterrence policy. She brings these diverse areas of expertise to her analysis and has successfully accomplished that which, literally, only a handful of scholars has accomplished in the past almost half century — an analysis that reflects fluency in both moral analysis and nuclear deterrence policy.

Using the centuries-old Just War Doctrine and more recent Law of Armed Conflict as the moral and legal frameworks for discussion, Dr. Heinrichs has rigorously and unflinchingly examined the morality of nuclear deterrence, not in a contextual vacuum, but in full recognition of the harsh realities of international relations. The result is a uniquely valuable contemporary assessment for a new generation of policy makers and operators that applies the Just War Doctrine and legal principles to current questions of nuclear deterrence and possible employment options.

The historical backdrop for Dr. Heinrichs' study is important to understanding its value. During the 1980s, there was a flowering of analyses and commentary in the West on this subject, including by numerous church-based authors and institutions. This flowering received considerable attention but demonstrated decidedly mixed levels of expertise on the primary subjects. The majority of these works reached one of two conclusions: 1) neither the possession nor employment of nuclear weapons can be deemed moral, and correspondingly, policies of nuclear deterrence must be rejected, or; 2) the possession of nuclear weapons *for deterrence purposes* may be morally acceptable pending their elimination under global surveillance and supervision, but *not* the employment of nuclear weapons. Two prominent Christian writers at the time went so far as to describe analysis advancing nuclear deterrence as "Satanic doublethink"[1]—the strongest possible denunciation.

In contrast, a distinct minority of these 1980s analyses concluded that the possession of nuclear weapons for deterrence purposes is a moral and strategic requirement

---

[1] Ronald Sider and Richard Taylor, *Nuclear Holocaust & Christian Hope* (Downers Grove, IL: InterVarsity Press, 1982), p. 69.

for the U.S. government—compatible with the Just War Doctrine—as are some prospective employment options in the event deterrence fails.

The rejection of nuclear deterrence as inherently immoral was wholly contrary to long-standing U.S. nuclear policies intended to deter war with the Soviet Union. When 1980s studies by church-based institutions reached this conclusion, the Reagan Administration took note for fear of the possible departure of pious professionals from U.S. efforts to sustain nuclear deterrence against the Soviet Union. Nevertheless, formal entry into this public debate by the Reagan Administration was limited. Instead, open argument against the moral rejection of nuclear deterrence fell to a small number of prominent scholars of the time, including Colin Gray, Herman Kahn, William O'Brien, and Albert Wohlstetter.

With the close of the Reagan Administration, voguish moral criticism of U.S. nuclear deterrence policy subsided. And, less than a decade later, the subject largely disappeared altogether from public discussion with the end of the Cold War and the widespread expectation of a cooperative "new world order" in which nuclear weapons and deterrence would be relics of the past.

The decades-long, post-Cold War quiet on the subject came to an end in 2017 with the United Nations' Treaty to Prohibit Nuclear Weapons (TPNW). A coalition of activist organizations promoting the TPNW, the International Campaign to Abolish Nuclear Weapons (ICAN), typically expressed emotive, moral outrage against nuclear weapons and deterrence rather than analytical arguments. This advocacy on behalf of the TPNW was, and typically remains, narrowly focused on the risks of nuclear deterrence and, on that basis, declares it to be inherently immoral.

Missing from this advocacy is any apparent acknowledgement of the realities of international threats and the risks associated with an absence of nuclear deterrence—risks illustrated during the first half of the 20th Century by the 80-100 million deaths from undeterred great power wars. In 2017, the Nobel Prize Committee awarded the Nobel Peace Prize to ICAN for its lobbying on behalf of the TPNW that is unburdened by recognition of the need to deter increasingly severe nuclear threats.

Several geopolitical developments have roughly coincided with this ICAN advocacy and contributed to the revival of interest in the moral and legal analysis of nuclear deterrence. Russia, intent on recovering the power position of the collapsed Soviet Union, has expanded its nuclear arsenal and increasingly engaged in reckless, explicit nuclear threats, as has North Korea. China too is expanding its nuclear capabilities and pursuing a manifestly aggressive foreign policy in the Indo-Pacific area. Initially slow to move in the direction of renewed nuclear capabilities, the United States established a program to rebuild its aged nuclear arsenal. In this darkening international context, the public debate about morality and nuclear deterrence has returned.

It is in this political context that Dr. Heinrichs' new contribution to the discussion of morality and nuclear deterrence has such meaning and value. Indeed, she rightly emphasizes that both moral and strategic analyses of nuclear weapons cannot be done adequately in a political vacuum. An understanding of the international threat context and the stakes at risk is essential: If there were no grave threats to be deterred confronting the United States and allies, it would be a simple matter to conclude that policies of nuclear deterrence provide no protection and instead entail only deadly risk—and therefore cannot be morally condoned. But, as Dr. Heinrichs explains, such international amity is not the reality, the current threat context is particularly harsh, and nuclear deterrence provides unique value to prevent war.

While acknowledging the risks of nuclear deterrence, Dr. Heinrichs meticulously takes the reader through a moral and strategic analysis that reaches a conclusion that is anathema to the secular activism in favor of the TPNW and contrary to much of the church-based analysis clothed in the Just War Doctrine: Policies of nuclear deterrence can be deemed strategically essential and fashioned to meet the strict demands of the Just War Doctrine regarding *jus ad bellum* and *jus in bello,* i.e., the decision to use force and its actual employment. The entire artifice of the nuclear disarmament campaign is built on the arguments that nuclear weapons and deterrence are inherently immoral and harmful; Dr. Heinrichs' careful analysis persuasively concludes that sustaining nuclear deterrence not only can be moral, but is Washington's sacred duty, and that U.S. nuclear policy has been moving in the direction demanded by the Just War Doctrine and legal principles for decades.

This conclusion is profoundly counter to most of the church-based and secular commentary on the subject— commentary that typically refuses to acknowledge the manifest dangers absent nuclear deterrence in the real world. The result of Dr. Heinrichs' timely analysis is a valuable and near unique text that is carefully reasoned, scholarly and readable, and directly pertinent to contemporary questions of nuclear weapons policy.

Duty to Deter truly is a must read for anyone interested in this critical subject, but particularly so for those in government and uniform with responsibility for U.S. deterrence policy and strategy. As Dr. Heinrichs concludes, those working to help sustain U.S. nuclear deterrence strategies and capabilities can do so confident that they are contributing to an undertaking that is both moral and a fundamental responsibility of government. *Duty to Deter* also is essential reading for members of the clergy and laypersons seeking a scholarly analysis informed by the needed expertise for such a study, and by recognition of both the risks of nuclear deterrence and its value given the harsh realities of international relations.

Dr. Keith B. Payne
Professor Emeritus of Defense and Strategic Studies
Missouri State University

Executive Summary

We are entering a new cold war era and adversaries are once again threatening to break the nuclear peace. That is true after almost four decades since the end of the first Cold War era, despite the progress of technology and human achievement and a more highly integrated global economy. American initiatives since the height of the Cold War to "lead the world" to lower the number of nuclear weapons worldwide and to prevent non-nuclear countries from acquiring or developing nuclear weapons may have contributed to non-proliferation goals, but they have not led to lasting stability or moved us closer to global nuclear zero. Despite U.S. initiatives to divest of certain categories of nuclear weapons, to unilaterally place restrictions on nuclear testing and design, and to place great importance on negotiating international arms control and disarmament efforts, the risk of nuclear war persists.

Current events have forced the subject of nuclear weapons back into the general public's consciousness. On February 24, 2022, Russia- the country with the world's most numerous nuclear arsenal- initiated the largest European war since 1945, expanded its assault against Ukraine, and threatened NATO with unleashing nuclear weapons. Though Russian president Vladimir Putin has not detonated a nuclear weapon, he used, and continues to use, his large nuclear arsenal to coerce the United States, Europe, and other nations against continuing to support Ukraine's defense.[2] Through nuclear saber-rattling, including verbally

---

[2] For further discussion see testimony of Mark A. Milley, USA, Chairman of the Joint Chiefs of Staff, before the House Armed Services Committee, March 29, 2023, available at https://armedservices.house.gov/sites/republicans.armedservices.hou se.gov/files/03.29.23%20Milley%20Statement.pdf.

threatening to employ nuclear weapons on the battlefield,[3] and putting such weapons on alert,[4] Russia caused President Joe Biden and his administration officials to declare repeatedly their fears of "World War III"[5] and to adopt a gradual, cautious approach to arming Ukraine. The White House has chosen to provide only weapons suitable for operations to allow Ukraine to achieve some tactical victories and prevent Russia from a quick and final victory,[6] but this aid, provided with many restrictions, has not equipped Ukraine to achieve and sustain the military victories necessary to repel Russia's invasion and occupation. Thus, Russia appears to have successfully used nuclear threats to deter the United States from certain actions that are on lower levels on the spectrum of escalation, enabling itself to control escalation to serve its aims. Russian officials have ample grounds to conclude that their nuclear coercion has affected the course of the war in their favor.

As yet, Russia has chosen to withhold employing nuclear weapons or escalating the war to include an attack on a NATO nation. So, while the United States was not successful in deterring Russia from invading Ukraine, and

---

[3] Vladimir Putin, "Message from the President of the Russian Federation," President of Russia, September 21, 2022, http://kremlin.ru/events/president/news/69390.

[4] Yuras Karmanau, Jim Heintz, Vladimir Isachenkov, and Dasha Litvinova, "Putin Puts Nuclear Forces on High Alert, Escalating Tensions," *AP*, February 27, 2022, available at https://apnews.com/article/russia-ukraine-kyiv-business-europe-moscow-2e4e1cf784f22b6afbe5a2f936725550.

[5] Josh Wingrove, "Biden Says He'd Fight World War III for NATO But Not for Ukraine," *Bloomberg*, March 11, 2022, https://www.bloomberg.com/news/articles/2022-03-11/biden-says-he-d-fight-world-war-iii-for-nato-but-not-for-ukraine.

[6] Rebeccah L. Heinrichs, "Biden's Risk Aversion is Escalating Putin's War," *Washington Examiner*, March 17, 2022, https://www.washingtonexaminer.com/opinion/bidens-risk-aversion-is-escalating-putins-war.

Russia has been successful in deterring the United States from sufficiently bolstering Ukraine's defense, the United States appears to have been successful in deterring Russia from crossing the nuclear threshold or escalating the war horizontally to attack a member of the NATO alliance. The challenge before the United States is to lessen the effectiveness of Moscow's nuclear coercion, to bolster the U.S. ability to provide necessary aid to allies under attack, and to credibly deter Russia from crossing the nuclear threshold.

Russia's nuclear threats before and during its 2022 conventional invasion of Ukraine are consistent with official assessments during the Trump Administration in the years prior to Russia's decision to invade. The 2018 *Nuclear Posture Review* says, "Moscow threatens and exercises [i.e., rehearses] limited nuclear first use, suggesting a mistaken expectation that coercive nuclear threats or limited first use could paralyze the United States and NATO and thereby end a conflict on terms favorable to Russia."[7] This strategy suits its numerically large arsenal of theater-range nuclear weapons, which Russia has refused to include in arms control restraints. Putin has also stopped complying with at least the verification provisions of the New START Treaty,[8] effectively ending the arms control treaty between Russia and the United States that is set to expire in February of 2026. The Russian decision to suspend the New START Treaty comes at an inauspicious time when, according to public U.S. government documents, Russia has sought a thorough nuclear

---

[7] U.S. Department of Defense, *Nuclear Posture Review* (Washington, D.C.: Department of Defense, 2018), p. 8, available at https://media.defense.gov/2018/Feb/02/2001872886/-1/-1/1/2018-NUCLEAR-POSTURE-REVIEW-FINAL-REPORT.PDF.

[8] U.S. Department of State, "Russian Noncompliance with and Invalid Suspension of the New START Treaty," *State.gov,* June 1, 2023, available at https://www.state.gov/russian-noncompliance-with-and-invalid-suspension-of-the-new-start-treaty/.

modernization program. Its modernization program has included enhancing its nuclear warhead production capacity, upgrades to its strategic delivery systems, and the development of novel systems of intercontinental range, as well as nuclear-powered undersea torpedoes.[9]

Like Russia, China is undertaking a significant nuclear weapons investment, modernization, and expansion project. It is increasing the number of its diverse nuclear force, has a nuclear triad (that is, a force with nuclear delivery systems including land-based intercontinental ballistic missiles, submarine-launched ballistic missiles, and heavy bombers that can carry bombs or missiles), and is developing defenses to protect its nuclear forces from being successfully targeted. The 2023 bipartisan U.S. Strategic Posture Commission concluded, "China is pursuing a nuclear force build-up on a scale and pace unseen since the U.S.-Soviet nuclear arms race that ended in the late 1980s."[10]

China has deployed a nuclear-capable precision-guided DF-26 intermediate-range ballistic missile (IRBM) capable of hitting targets on land and or at sea. As of October 2022, according to the Commander of U.S. Strategic Command, General Anthony Cotton, China's inventory of land-based fixed and mobile ICBM launchers "exceeds the number of ICBM launchers in the United States."[11] According to the Pentagon, if China continues the pace of its nuclear expansion, it will likely field a stockpile of about 1,500

---

[9] U.S. Department of Defense, *2018 Nuclear Posture Review*, op. cit., p. 9.

[10] Congressional Commission on the Strategic Posture of the United States, *America's Strategic Posture: The Final Report of the Congressional Commission on the Strategic Posture of the United States*, p. 8, available at strategic-posture-commission-report.ashx (ida.org).

[11] Michael R. Gordon, "China Has More ICBM Launchers Than U.S., American Military Reports," *The Wall Street Journal*, February 7, 2023, available at https://www.wsj.com/articles/china-has-more-icbm-launchers-than-u-s-american-military-reports-11675779463.

nuclear warheads by 2035.[12] On March 9, 2022, the then-Commander of U.S. Strategic Command Admiral Charles Richard, testified before the Senate Armed Services Committee:

> Today, we face two nuclear capable near peers who have the capability to unilaterally escalate to any level of violence in any domain worldwide with any instrument of national power at any time. And we have never faced the situation before like that in our history. Last fall, I formally reported to the Secretary of Defense, the PRC strategic breakout.[13]

Richard went on to testify, "Today's nuclear force is the minimum required to achieve our national strategy. Right now, I am executing my strategic deterrence mission under historic stress crisis levels of deterrence, crisis deterrence dynamics, that we've only seen a couple of times in our nation's history."[14]

Those "historic stress crisis levels of deterrence" are perceptible even to civilians, and Americans are right to ask their government about its plans to protect the country. Especially in a republic such as the United States, the government should be prepared to explain the dangers and its plans to mitigate or defeat them. In the modern era with a saturated information space and democratized "news

---

[12] U.S. Department of Defense, *Military and Security Developments Involving the People's Republic of China* (Washington, D.C.: Department of Defense, 2022), p. 98, available at https://media.defense.gov/2022/Nov/29/2003122279/-1/-1/1/2022-MILITARY-AND-SECURITY-DEVELOPMENTS-INVOLVING-THE-PEOPLES-REPUBLIC-OF-CHINA.PDF.

[13] Charles Richard, "U.S. Strategic Command and U.S. Space Command SASC Testimony" *Stratcom.mil*, March 9, 2022, available at https://www.stratcom.mil/Media/Speeches/Article/2960836/us-strategic-command-and-us-space-command-sasc-testimony/.

[14] Ibid.

sources" Americans may develop views gleaned from legacy media or social media influencers, some sources about the impact America's nuclear weapons have on the world, whether the U.S. nuclear posture is optimally suited to protect them, and if it comports with their understanding of morality. As Christian realist Paul Ramsey (dubbed "the most important Protestant writer on war in the 1950s and 1960s"[15] by social scientist Michael Walzer) exhorts, "Every citizen must make up his part of the public-policy decision. He is a lesser magistrate. He has his particular measure of jurisdictional competence to think through to the end an application of the moral principles governing political action. Let us hope he has the actual competence to do this."[16] The purpose of this study is to aid in equipping the private citizen and policymaker with such competence.

Towards that end, this study is focused on informing an answer to the important question: is it possible for the United States to embrace a nuclear deterrence posture that is moral? The study's method for evaluating this question is to first identify the Just War Doctrine (JWD) as a sound standard of measurement for morality in nuclear deterrence. The JWD's enormous impact on U.S. and international law underscores its salience, as does its direct impact on widely accepted ethical standards such as the Law of Armed Conflict (LOAC) and the U.S. guidance for implementation of the LOAC in the Department of Defense *Law of War Manual.*

The study goes on to assess the idealist and realist frameworks for international relations. This is important for the study's purposes because scholars who appeal to matters of ethics or morality are often assumed to be

---

[15] Michael Walzer, *Just and Unjust Wars: A Moral Argument with Historical Illustrations* (New York: Basic Books, 1977, fifth edition) p. 336.

[16] Paul Ramsey, *The Just War: Force and Political Responsibility* (New York: Charles Scribner's Sons, 1966), p. 338.

idealists. And if they are idealists, there may be a temptation to write off their judgments about strategy and security. But assuming a strategist who makes appeals to morality is an idealist is a category error with consequences. After analyzing the assumptions of realists and the JWD, the study will show that many JWD scholars are best understood as belonging to the realist school. As it relates to policies within the field of nuclear deterrence and disarmament, it is important to establish that the assumptions that provide the basis of the JWD are at odds with the assumptions that form the basis of the idealist framework; instead, they remain salient guides for nuclear deterrence and strategy within a realist framework.

The study then seeks to apply the main principles of the JWD, as outlined by its most prominent scholars, to nuclear deterrence strategy and the logic of deterrence. The study does not explore the nuances of the rich theology that shapes the JWD or its historical development, but it will address the common precepts upon which JWD scholars agree, and from which they derive those JWD principles. The study will not give full treatment to the universe of nuances among JWD scholars; doing so would warrant a separate study. Rather, it seeks to bring to bear only the most fundamental points that scholars of the JWD consistently make and that are pertinent to the questions the study seeks to answer. Some of those scholars are patriarchs of JWD such as Saints Ambrose, Aquinas, and Augustine, as well as Protestant giants Martin Luther, John Calvin, and more modern scholars including Paul Ramsay, William O'Brien, Jean Bethke Elshtain, and Reinhold Niebuhr. The JWD's 1,600-year institutional Christian embrace across Catholicism and Protestantism is a testament to its lasting ecumenical appeal and its tested durability spanning centuries under the rigorous study of devoted theologians and ethicists.

The questions addressed here are meant to drive discoveries about the JWD, the atomic age, and to answer whether a country like the United States that professes a just and humane system of government and a world order that seeks to promote and adhere to certain moral precepts can claim a moral defense of its nuclear deterrence approach.

It is common for activists who warn about the threat of nuclear war, especially those who address nuclear weapons from a moral or ethical perspective, to argue quite emotionally against amending the U.S. strategic posture in a way that strengthens U.S. deterrent capabilities, adding more capable active defenses, or providing the United States with more potential nuclear response options if deterrence fails. The reason for this opposition often stems from a fear of provoking "strategic instability" and a subsequent arms race. For these activists, the only way to be morally upright is for the United States to lead the world towards global nuclear disarmament or to support a nuclear weapons global ban. Examining the assumptions and logic of these arguments, which activists and theologians have put forward since the Cold War, is essential for equipping the strategist and citizen with the ability to discern and think more clearly about the morality of U.S. deterrence strategy.

Due to the prominence of nuclear pacifism, that is, the approval of possessing nuclear weapons for deterrence but never of nuclear weapons employment if deterrence fails, it is important to assess the argument Christian scholars make for it. The study will pay special attention to, for example, the influential 1983 National Conference on Catholic Bishops pastoral letter, "The Challenge of Peace: God's Promise and Our Response." It will also examine arguments of those who go further than those who accept nuclear weapons for deterrence purposes but never for use. It will consider the views of those who reject even a policy of deterrence in favor of total nuclear disarmament, such as the arguments found in the 1982 book *Nuclear Holocaust and Christian Hope: A Book for Christian Peacemakers* by Ronald Sider and Richard Taylor.

Drawing on the study's discussion of the JWD and the realist international relations framework, it also will trace the logic of those who make JWD arguments *against* total nuclear disarmament and *against* nuclear pacifism, for example, the logic of the arguments articulated by William O'Brien and Keith Payne.[17]

There are other pressing matters related to nuclear weapons and security that are worthy of detailed exploration: issues such as extended nuclear deterrence and the assurance of U.S. allies and the wisdom of working towards nuclear nonproliferation. While the study does note these issues as they relate to the questions it addresses, they are more tangential to the study's focus. However, the findings of this study could be applied to these other aspects of nuclear policy. The study also does not provide a comprehensive treatment of the various schools of thought in nuclear deterrence, but a keen student of nuclear strategy will observe the influence of prominent nuclear strategists such as Herman Kahn, Thomas Schelling, Kenneth Waltz, Albert Wohlstetter, and Colin Gray.

The study concludes with the following findings: Contrary to those who argue that morality requires the United States to pursue immediate nuclear disarmament and a posture of nuclear pacifism, the JWD precludes both. The United States has a moral duty to protect the innocent and punish the adversary, which motivates its Constitutional obligation to provide for the common defense.

---

[17] See for example, William O'Brien's seminal 2007 essay, William V. O'Brien, "The Bishops' Unfinished Business," *Comparative Strategy*, Vol. 5, No. 2 (1985) and the classic 1988 essay by Keith B. Payne and Jill E. Coleman, "Christian Nuclear Pacifism and Just War Theory: Are They Compatible?" *Comparative Strategy*, Vol. 7, No. 1 (Winter 1988).

Especially in the atomic age when the United States faces two major nuclear adversaries with imperialist aims, when acts of aggression with conventional weapons have the potential to precipitate actions that could escalate to include crossing the nuclear threshold,[18] deterring adversaries from choosing nuclear or massive conventional attack in pursuit of their goals is the highest and most important task of U.S. strategic deterrence. The stakes are enormously high, and with it, the duty to deter adversaries becomes greater.

What morality demands of the just warrior (and citizen of a democratic republic) is far more than a sincere *desire* to maintain peace and do justice or a sincere *desire* to refrain from committing injustice; morality demands just intent and *affecting just outcomes*. The justice of a national policy must be measured against its intent and outcomes. Nuclear disarmament and nuclear pacifism, even if sincerely well-intended to achieve peace, present an unacceptably high risk of precipitating grave injustice on a catastrophic scale.

Deterring an aggressor from committing harm against innocents is the primary aim of American strategic deterrence policy. Causing the adversary to believe that it

---

[18] For additional information, see Rebeccah L. Heinrichs, "Deter Conventional Wars to Avoid the Nuclear Precipice" *Providence Magazine*, January 5, 2023, available at https://providencemag.com/2023/01/deter-conventional-wars-to-avoid-nuclear-precipice/, which quotes William O'Brien writing in 1984, "The greatest threats to the free world do not arise from the possibility of a Soviet nuclear 'bolt from the blue' attack on the United States. For the present, the greatest threats are not posed by the contingency of a blatant attack on NATO. As Henry Kissinger was already pointing out in 1957, the greatest threats are likely to come in areas sufficiently important to be defended but just sufficiently marginal and inconvenient geopolitically that it may be difficult to marshal the free world resistance aggression against them. In such cases the possibilities of misperceptions and accidents may abound, and it is there that nuclear war may occur, arising out of a confused and unsuccessful conventional defense."

would not prevail against the United States, and that the cost of attacking U.S. interests would far outweigh the potential gain, is the nature of U.S. deterrence policy. Strategic deterrence relies on adversaries' sufficient belief that the United States can hold at risk what the adversary values most and possesses the will to employ the most powerful weapons to achieve this end if necessary. The nature of the adversary and the dynamic target sets it possesses rightly drive U.S. strategic deterrence requirements. As the United States sought to adapt its strategic deterrence requirements in the 1970s, to make deterrence policy more credible, the policy underwent a significant change.

The 1973 Foster Commission Report helped cement what has become lasting and persistent categories of targets for deterrence purposes: the enemy regime and its control apparatus, its conventional and nuclear capabilities, and its means of post-war recovery to continue its aggression against the United States.[19] Over the span of Republican and Democratic administrations since the Cold War, the United States has adapted U.S. deterrence options to enhance the credibility of deterrence, to refine its nuclear strategy, and it

---

[19] Summary Report of the Inter-Agency Working Group on NSSM 169 (Washington, D.C.: The White House, June 1973), p. 14, originally Top Secret, now declassified, available at https://nsarchive2.gwu.edu/NSAEBB/NSAEBB173/SIOP-21.pdf, (Hereafter, *the Foster Panel Report*). The author would like to thank Matthew Costlow for his guidance in establishing this report as foundational to understanding established U.S. nuclear policy and as the intellectual grandfather of key policy documents such as NSDM-242, PD-59, and NSDD-13; for a great explanation of the importance of the Foster Panel, see Keith B. Payne and Matthew R. Costlow, "Back to the Future: U.S. Nuclear Deterrence Today and the Foster Panel Study," *Information Series*, No. 565 (Fairfax, VA: National Institute Press, October 16, 2023), available at https://nipp.org/information_series/keith-b-payne-and-matthew-r-costlow-back-to-the-future-u-s-nuclear-deterrence-today-and-the-foster-panel-study-no-565-october-16-2023/.

should continue to do so as the threats evolve. But the deterrence paradigm, to hold at risk what the enemy regime values, to optimize the safety of Americans and allies through, for instance, active defenses, and to not attack civilians and societal targets as such, remains unchanging.

As the global dynamics change, it is morally licit — and indeed, a moral duty — for the United States to adapt its nuclear deterrence options and posture as needed to credibly meet its deterrence requirements, maintain just order, and protect the innocent. Furthermore, the United States should, with appropriate humility, prepare for the possibility that deterrence may fail. This possibility compels the just strategist to continue to develop and deploy a defense of Americans, while seeking to target only what the enemy regime values and not innocents, to seek to limit the levels of violence perpetrated against innocents, and to endeavor to pressure the enemy to return to a state of peace on terms favorable to the United States as quickly as possible. Adapting U.S. deterrence options to meet deterrence requirements can mean making weapons more survivable, accurate, lethal, deployed in different locations, and more numerous. It also may drive an investment in weapons that minimize the risk to the defender such as stand-off capabilities, adding stealth technology, and better and more numerous active defenses to protect innocent Americans and preserve U.S. options steer the adversary to cease attacks and accept an outcome that advantages Americans.

The United States has indeed pursued such investments and adapted the emphasis it places on offensive and defensive complementary systems. To develop deterrence policy and planning to ensure its appropriate credibility since the mid-1970s, it has, remarkably, also moved increasingly in congruence with the JWD. This supports the position that adapting nuclear deterrence options with the primary focus to strengthen the credibility of deterrence can also be consistent with the principles of the JWD. Preparing to prevail against adversaries if deterrence fails and conflict ensues likewise strengthens the credibility of the deterrence posture and also seeks to limit damage and optimally protect innocents from harm, consistent with the principles of the JWD.

Until deterrence is no longer needed to prevent large-scale conventional or nuclear attack, adopting a policy view that forecloses or restricts the United States from improving the credibility of U.S. deterrence and instead embraces policy proposals on a path towards nuclear disarmament, in the absence of an unexpected and radical change in the international security environment, would violate the JWD in both means and outcomes.

It would violate the JWD by potentially causing an adversary to believe it can attack the United States at an acceptable cost, thereby tempting deterrence failure. And once deterrence has failed, the U.S. failure to prepare options for limited response against military and regime targets would leave the United States only with options to inflict violence and destruction on a larger scale and with greater civilian death and suffering. Last, by failing to invest in adequate defenses as a key aspect of strategic deterrence, the United States would leave innocent Americans vulnerable to undeterred attacks of the aggressor, with little ability to limit damage or stop a determined adversary from imposing grave harm against innocents, including societal destruction and tyranny. The task before us is not to rethink deterrence or reject deterrence principles that have been in place throughout the nuclear age. The great task is to relearn deterrence, embrace those principles, and further adapt the deterrent posture to bolster its credibility as a matter of national security necessity and moral duty.

Introduction

Almost four decades since the end of the Cold War, the United States once again faces grave threats to its security and way of life. Two top-tier strategic adversaries, the Peoples Republic of China (PRC) and the Russian Federation, are highly motivated to replace the United States and the U.S. alliance architectures, laws, and standards between and among nations that have benefited American freedom, security, and prosperity since the Second World War. At the same time, the PRC and Russia are investing in their militaries and, notably, their nuclear weapons programs.

The Russian Federation is about to complete a significant nuclear modernization program. It has developed novel strategic systems. And Russia remains unwilling to restrain its theater-range nuclear weapons by arms control measures and is developing and fielding several thousand theater-range warheads on a spectrum of delivery systems reportedly for credible employment.[20] Russia is also threatening to employ nuclear weapons in a conventional war it chose against Ukraine to deter the United States from backing Ukraine "too much." This concept of threatening to employ a nuclear weapon in a purely conventional conflict to terminate the conflict, has been described in public U.S. military documents as a possible official Russian doctrine.[21] Senior military officials

---

[20] Christopher Yeaw, "To Deter China, Invest in Non-Strategic Nuclear Weapons," *Real Clear Defense*, December 4, 2021, available at https://www.realcleardefense.com/articles/2021/12/04/to_deter_chin a_invest_in_non-strategic_nuclear_weapons_806401.html.

[21] Defense Intelligence Agency, *Russia Military Power: Building a Military to Support Great Power Aspirations* (Washington, D.C.: Defense Intelligence Agency, 2017), p. 22, available at https://info.publicintelligence.net/DIA-RussiaMilitaryPower2017.pdf.

have gone further in their own professional assessments and have described Russian doctrine as "escalate-to-win."[22]

The PRC is amid a significant nuclear weapons program investment, is expanding its ability to produce nuclear warheads, and is engaged in what former U.S. Strategic Command Commander Admiral Charles "Chas" Richard called a "strategic breakout."[23] China is also diversifying its ability to deliver nuclear weapons, including through a nuclear triad of delivery systems. Then-Commander of U.S. Strategic Command Admiral Richard issued a dire warning: "As I assess our level of deterrence against China, the ship is slowly sinking... As these curves keep going, it isn't going to matter how good our (operating plan) is or how good our commanders are, or how good our forces are—we're not going to have enough of them."[24]

Those top tier strategic foes have the greatest potential to do the greatest harm, but they are not the only ones that seek to harm the United States. Rogue nation North Korea has nuclear intercontinental ballistic missiles (ICBMs) and

---

[22] For clarification of this concept of "escalating to win" in the context of Russian possible employment of tactical nuclear weapons, see Charles Richard, USSTRATCOM Commander, "U.S. Strategic Command and U.S. Space Command SASC Testimony" *Stratcom.mil*, April 21, 2021, available at
https://www.stratcom.mil/Media/Speeches/Article/2960836/us-strategic-command-and-us-space-command-sasc-testimony/.

[23] Aaron Mehta, "STRATCOM Chief Warns of Chinese 'Strategic Breakout,'" *Breaking Defense*, August 12, 2021, available at https://breakingdefense.com/2021/08/stratcom-chief-warns-of-chinese-strategic-breakout/.

[24] Quoted in, C. Todd Lopez, "Stratcom Commander Says U.S. Should Look to 1959s to Regain Competitive Edge," U.S. Department of Defense, November 3, 2022, available at https://www.defense.gov/News/News-Stories/Article/Article/3209416/stratcom-commander-says-us-should-look-to-1950s-to-regain-competitive-edge/.

continues to improve its nuclear weapons arsenal,[25] and potential nuclear adversary Iran poses serious threats to U.S. interests in the Middle East and has the potential to develop a nuclear-armed ICBM. The PRC and Russia are increasingly leveraging North Korea and Iran to further their malign aims to undermine the United States and our allies. Adding complexity to the challenge for defense planners, Xi Jinping and Vladimir Putin are increasing their collaboration in troubling ways.[26]

As reports of nuclear adversaries testing, brandishing, and threatening to employ nuclear weapons appear with increasing frequency in the news media, the topic of nuclear weapons and the fear of nuclear war have returned to the public's consciousness. Civic and religious organizations as well as analysts offer commentary about how the United States should respond, appealing to prominent religious publications or the logic of arguments that were popular during the Cold War era.

Meanwhile, U.S. government military strategists work to devise plans for how best to credibly deter the adversaries threatening the United States in compliance with legal guidance. The American people, most of whom are neither trained religious scholars and ethicists nor military strategists, may wonder if U.S. defense policy as it relates to the most powerful categories of weapons is compatible with their view of ethics and morality. Especially in a republic governed democratically, American citizens should be informed and confident in the effectiveness of their deterrence options and have clarity

---

[25] Mary Beth D. Nikitin, "North Korea's Nuclear Weapons and Missile Programs," *Congressional Research Service,* January 23, 2023, available at https://crsreports.congress.gov/product/pdf/IF/IF10472/23.

[26] David Vergun, "Russia Reportedly Supplying Enriched Uranium to China," *DOD News,* March 8, 2023, available at https://www.defense.gov/News/News-Stories/Article/Article/3323381/russia-reportedly-supplying-enriched-uranium-to-china/.

about the moral uprightness of their military plans. The question about the morality of U.S. nuclear deterrence is therefore a salient one, and one that deserves a serious analytical treatment applied to the modern context.

The U.S. Constitution is the paramount legal document that obligates the federal government to provide for the common defense. But how the United States does that is dynamic. Changes in the relations among nations—both allies and adversaries—the advancement of technology, and the investments in different categories of weapons manifest new challenges for policymakers. Despite these challenges, the United States has sought to formulate ethical and legal guidelines and duties as they pertain to warfighting since the earliest days of the Republic.

Today they are codified in the Law of Armed Conflict (LOAC). The LOAC is a collection of treaties and customary international law that establishes international standards for ethical behavior in war that are meant to prevent excessive human suffering and civilizational destruction. The LOAC proffers principles that ought to guide ethical conduct in war including the distinction between civilians and combatants, the military necessity of violence, and taking precautionary measures to avoid inflicting unnecessary suffering.[27] U.S. military forces are not subject to the adjudication of the International Criminal Court (ICC). Choosing to not become a state party to the Rome Statute of the ICC has been affirmed by Republican and Democratic administrations as a matter of retaining U.S. national sovereignty. U.S. military forces are required to operate in accordance with U.S. legal interpretations of the LOAC and may be held liable in the United States for

---

[27] Bryan Frederick and David E. Johnson, "The Continued Evolution of U.S. Law of Armed Conflict Implementation; Implications for the U.S. Military," *RAND Corporation*, 2015, available at https://www.rand.org/content/dam/rand/pubs/research_reports/R R1100/RR1122/RAND_RR1122.pdf.

specific violations of the Uniform Code of Military Justice (UCMJ) and the War Crimes Act of 1996.

To interpret U.S. legal stipulations, and to guide, set boundaries, and clarify obligations on the conduct of American forces, the Department of Defense issued the *Law of War Manual*. Much of the *Law of War Manual* is separate from but directly influenced by and even rooted in the JWD. The *Law of War Manual* explicitly acknowledges that nuclear weapons policy remains tethered to JWD principles.[28] Importantly, the *Laws of War Manual* applies to the use of all categories of weapons, whether conventional or nuclear weapons.[29]

U.S. legal instructions and training aside, some prominent religious leaders have questioned whether the atomic age has simply obviated the application of the JWD, and whether the JWD permits even nuclear weapons possession for deterrence purposes only or whether there is ever a morally licit reason for possible employment if deterrence fails. There are prominent thinkers who embrace the JWD and who conclude that no just government can ever possess or employ nuclear weapons; and there are other influential thinkers who have concluded that the JWD permits possessing nuclear weapons for deterrence purposes only, but not for employment.

It is common to find those who make moral arguments about nuclear weapons to argue that one must generally oppose them, oppose U.S. efforts to modernize or otherwise improve them, and to support the cause of moving towards total global nuclear disarmament. Among the heritage of

---

[28] U.S. Department of Defense, *Law of War Manual*, (Washington, D.C.: DoD Office of General Counsel, June 2015 (updated December 2016), p. 26, available at https://dod.defense.gov/Portals/1/Documents/pubs/DoD%20Law%20of%20War%20Manual%20-%20June%202015%20Updated%20Dec%202016.pdf?ver=2016-12-13-172036-190

[29] Ibid., p. 417.

religious commentary about nuclear weapons and U.S. deterrence, there is a strong bias against all nuclear weapons, including U.S. nuclear weapons, a fear of arms racing, handwringing over U.S. nuclear deterrence signaling, and an outright opposition to investing in strategic forces modernization and adaptation.

For example, after World War II, the World Council of Churches and National Council of Churches encompassing the mainline Protestant churches, lobbied against nuclear testing and for nuclear disarmament.[30] The United Methodist Bishops pointedly called deterrence "idolatry."[31] In 1964 the Second Vatican Council discussed a statement on nuclear arms. The discussion was recorded in Article 25 of the "Schema XIII" and would inform the 1965 "Pastoral Constitution on the Church and the Modern World." In Article 25, it said that the effects of nuclear weapons "exceeds all just proportion and therefore must be judged before God and man as wicked."[32]

The sweeping opposition to nuclear weapons from prominent religious leaders was based on arguments that often point to, either implicitly or explicitly, the same few JWD principles that many theologians and their religious adherents believe the employment of nuclear weapons necessarily violates. Those principles are proportionality, discrimination, right intention, and probability of success. The last two principles, right intention and probability of success, are linked to claims about nuclear employment and the technical characteristics that opponents believe make

---

[30] See Peter Feaver, William Inboden, and Michael Singh, "What Christians Must Remember about Nuclear Weapons and Arms Control," *Providence Magazine*, June 8, 2020, available at https://providencemag.com/2020/06/what-christians-must-remember-nuclear-weapons-arms-control/.

[31] Quoted in Keith B. Payne and Jill E. Coleman, "Christian Nuclear Pacifism and The Just War Tradition," op. cit., p. 75.

[32] Paul Ramsey, *The Just War*, op. cit., p. 283.

them "inherently indiscriminate," and will necessarily lead to uncontrolled escalation to nuclear Armageddon, which leads to the violation of the principles of discrimination and proportionality. This study will put special focus on assessing analyses that lead to those prominent objections and the arguments and logic that dissent from them. The study will go on to identify policy implications of those assessments.

The Just War Doctrine

The JWD was developed primarily by religious scholars who hold to the realist assumptions that establish their outlook on international relations. That is, they understood that nations are fundamentally distrustful of one another, that nations generally prize their own security interests above all else, and that, in the words of the political philosopher and ethicist Jean Bethke Elshtain, appealing to St. Augustine, "the earthly city is never free from the dangers of bloodshed, sedition, and war."[33] War is not something that mankind can abolish any more than man can abolish his fallen human nature. At the same time, these religious scholars did not believe, as some realists would go on to do, that the reality of this unhappy human condition exempted Christians or non-religious but morally conscious people and nations from moral behavior and aims.[34] Thus, the JWD was developed to inform the consciences of

---

[33] Jean Bethke Elshtain, *Augustine and the Limits of Politics* (Notre Dame, IN: University of Notre Dame Press, 1995) p. 111.

[34] For additional discussion, see Elshtain's appeal to Augustinian scholarship about the need to have an accurate and low view of human nature while simultaneously aiming for limited and just war in accordance with the JWD in Jean Bethke Elshtain, "Peace, Order, Justice: Competing Understandings," *Millennium Journal of International Studies*, Vol. 36, No. 3 (2008), p. 421, available at https://journals.sagepub.com/doi/abs/10.1177/03058298080360030201.

Christians and equip them to discern the justice of, and justice in, war, and to help shape the standards for morally acceptable reasons to enter war and morally upright behavior in war.

For some activist organizations that reject realism and instead hold to an idealist international relations framework — such as the International Campaign to Abolish Nuclear Weapons (ICAN) — global nuclear disarmament is the imperative. Idealists may, like many JWD scholars, hold sincere religious convictions and concerns about justice among nations, but they are ill-suited to utilize the intellectual tools, so to speak, of the JWD because the JWD is useful within the framework of a realist view of reality and with a bounded view of what is humanly possible. Idealists hold out as a foreseeable goal the transformation of the contemporary global system to one of order, cooperation, amity and disarmament. This immediately sets them at odds with realists who do not believe the needed global transformation is humanly possible apart from a sudden unforeseen and unprecedented global event, or with religious realists who hold open the possibility of Divine action like the eschatological finale described in the Bible.[35] For the latter, the anticipation of the eventual

---

[35] See, for example, Daniel 12, which foretells the Second Coming of Christ and God's establishment of the New Heavens; or Isaiah 65:17-25 when the Prophet describes through beautiful imagery a utopian world God will wipe away every vestige of sin and its effects and "no more shall be heard in it the sound of weeping and the cry of distress... The wolf and the lamb shall graze together..."; or Acts 24:15 that exhorts a hope in God that He will fulfill His promise to perfectly issue final judgment on humanity; or Hebrews 9:27-28 which calls all who hope for salvation to persevere in this sinful and imperfect world waiting expectantly for perfect and final judgment; or Revelation 21:1-4, which describes "the new heave and the new earth" where God will "wipe away every year from their eyes, and death shall be no more, neither shall there be mourning, nor crying, nor pain anymore, for the former things have passed away."

Divinely appointed occurrences provide no basis for delaying or forgoing prudent national policy and planning.

Idealists view as within reach a harmonious world with a global governing institution able to arbitrate misunderstandings and disagreements among nations. Idealists tend to see efforts to build up arms as contrary to the global transformation they seek, are especially wary of "arms races," and view improvements to nuclear deterrence as an impediment to disarmament regardless of the activities of U.S. adversaries. These disarmament organizations often borrow arguments from religious groups and authors who make moral arguments in favor of nuclear disarmament.[36]

Beyond the insistence that there is a moral imperative for total nuclear disarmament, there is another influential religious argument that concludes that the United States can possess nuclear weapons for deterrence purposes but not for employment. This view, as is elaborated in this study, is effectively nuclear pacifism. Due to the influence of these two arguments—in favor of nuclear disarmament or nuclear pacifism—this study will pay special attention to assessing them.

One of the discoveries herein is that those who conclude the JWD requires the strategist to support nuclear disarmament or nuclear pacifism are, whether conscientiously or not, evaluating nuclear deterrence against the JWD principles according to standards that could only be met within the idealist international relations framework; however, to reiterate, the JWD is an amalgam of principles and thought predicated on the embrace of a realist framework. Trying to fit the JWD into the atomic age

---

[36] For a fuller treatment of the differences between realism and idealism and the implications of the difference, see Keith B. Payne, "Realism, Idealism, Deterrence, and Disarmament," *Strategic Studies Quarterly*, Vol. 13, No. 3 (Fall 2019), pp. 7-37, available at https://www.jstor.org/stable/26760126.

while holding presuppositions that are unique to an idealist framework for international relations will lead to incoherent and outright logical contradictions.

Not all religious scholars and nuclear theorists conclude that the JWD compels support for the disarmament agenda or nuclear pacifism. Some JWD scholars, who self-consciously hold to a realist international relations framework, conclude that it is possible to devise a nuclear deterrence strategy that satisfies the JWD principles and meets the requirements for deterrence. Indeed, careful examination of the JWD, as well as the historical evidence, and the logic of the arguments put forward by certain JWD strategists, leads to the conclusion that the Divinely appointed duty of the just government and the principles of justice *require* the United States to maintain and improve options for nuclear deterrence — including for achieving military aims if deterrence fails — as the dangers to innocents change over time. Scholars who dissented from the post-World War II Christian disarmers include prominent scholars like Protestant theologian and strategist Paul Ramsey,[37] whose canon of scholarly work on the JWD is significant and influential. Another critical dissenter of the disarmers was the original editor of the magazine *Christianity Today*, Carl F.H. Henry, who penned a famous essay in 1957 called "Christ and the Atom Bomb."[38] In it, Henry, a theologian who was active at the Metropolitan Baptist Church in Washington, DC, now called Capitol Hill Baptist Church, defended the U.S. possession and testing of its nuclear weapons arsenal on the grounds that the biblically assigned Divine duty of a civil government is to "promote justice and to restrain injustice in a sinful society,"

---

[37] Ramsey, *The Just War*, op. cit., p. 284.

[38] Carl F.H. Henry, "Christ and the Atom Bomb," *Christianity Today*, Vol. 1, No. 23 (September 2, 1957), available at
https://www.christianitytoday.com/ct/1957/september-2/editorials-christ-and-atom-bomb.html.

and that by failing to maintain credible deterrence, the United States would be surrendering to a Communist state that makes no pretense about the "goal of world revolution."

Two prominent scholars who are proficient in both the JWD and nuclear deterrence strategy who have come to this same conclusion are William O'Brien and Keith B. Payne.[39] No other writers have been so thorough and persistent in their scholarship and argumentation in this unique discipline spanning four decades.

It is important to examine the JWD principles and keep them in mind as strategists grapple with assessing the national wills and military capabilities of U.S. adversaries. Applying the LOAC in a dynamic environment when the adversary is changing behaviors and capabilities could lead U.S. strategists to adapt U.S. nuclear deterrence options and strategies, for example by adding supplemental delivery systems and warheads and improving active defenses. Failing to make needed adaptations risks missing opportunities to strengthen deterrence in ways that offer policymakers and military operators the confidence of moral clarity according to the JWD as embraced by the LOAC. This confidence, as wrought from a properly informed conscience, is an inherent good, but it can also be a powerful means of strengthening political resolve and in turn motivate behaviors that more convincingly communicate to the adversary the credibility of potential undesirable outcomes if it attacks U.S. interests.[40] Put

---

[39] Please see William V. O'Brien, *The Conduct of Just and Limited War* (New York, NY: Praeger, 1983); Keith B. Payne and Karl I. Payne, *A Just Defense* (Portland, OR: Multnomah Press, 1987), and; Keith B. Payne, *Chasing a Grand Illusion: Replacing Deterrence with Disarmament* (Fairfax, VA: National Institute Press, 2023).

[40]For further discussion see, Colin S. Gray, *Nuclear Strategy and Strategic Planning* (Philadelphia, PA: Foreign Policy Research Institute, 1984), p. 9. Colin Gray notes that an adversary's uncertainty about U.S.

simply, U.S. confidence in the justice of the U.S. nuclear deterrence strategy can strengthen the credibility of U.S. deterrence in the minds of the adversary. U.S. confidence in the justice of its nuclear deterrence strategy can help to dissuade adversaries from acting in harmful ways and steer them towards restraint, and thereby bolster the furtherance of the good (including the protection of the innocent) that is at the heart of the JWD. It also will help to facilitate the maintenance of allied support and cooperation as well as the domestic support in the United States necessary for investing in measures that sustain credible deterrence.

Conversely, assessing the question of "what is morally licit" incorrectly risks bruising the consciences of those policymakers, military strategists, and operators charged with the responsibility to design and carry out plans for deterrence, and to protect and prevail in a war if deterrence fails. Beyond this moral bruising, policymakers who reach fallacious conclusions in their response to the question of whether credible nuclear deterrence is morally licit risk conveying a shaky political resolve to adversaries, allies, and the American people. Making incorrect judgments about the morality of U.S. nuclear deterrence could also lead policymakers to make changes to the U.S. deterrence strategy or force posture, or to refuse to make needed changes, either of which could unintentionally invite military aggression, the prospect of major war, and leave America ill-equipped to prevail in war by ending the war on terms favorable to the United States.

---

behavior could strengthen deterrence, it can be taken too far. Gray instructs, "[T]he U.S. government should know what it is about. As a deterrent virtue, uncertainty can provide a too convenient cover for doctrinal confusion and muddled thinking."

U.S. Deterrence Adapts

It is for those reasons that this study seeks to answer the pressing and timely question: can the United States fulfil its Constitutional obligation to provide for the common defense in the modern nuclear threat context by maintaining a nuclear deterrence posture that credibly meets the deterrence objectives and is also morally righteous?

While seeking to answer that question, this study will focus on four areas, each one explored in a chapter; each chapter will build upon the previous one until the answer to the question comes into clear focus.

The first chapter will explore the reasons the JWD is a sound moral framework to evaluate the righteousness – the justice – of U.S. nuclear deterrence strategy. The second chapter will explore the provenance of the JWD, paying special notice to its place in the realist framework in international relations. In this chapter the study will also outline the principles of the JWD. The third chapter will analyze the way prominent theologians have applied the JWD to nuclear deterrence strategy and concluded that preparing to possibly employ nuclear weapons if deterrence fails as a means of restoring deterrence cannot meet one or all the JWD principles: discrimination, proportionality, probability of success, and right intention. The third chapter will also devote special attention to assessing influential arguments that insist that, because they conclude that nuclear deterrence fails to meet one or all the JWD principles, the just warrior ought to favor nuclear disarmament or nuclear pacifism.

The fourth chapter will investigate how U.S. nuclear deterrence policy and strategy have, since the early 1970s,[41] developed in a consistent direction. Presidents often carried

---

[41] NSSM-169, *the Foster Panel Report,* was a watershed moment in the history of U.S. nuclear strategy.

out very different foreign policies and approaches toward engagement or confrontation, but the foundation of their deterrence policies have consistently held to a common approach. Presidents and their strategists clarified, sharpened, and made more explicit the U.S. approach to nuclear deterrence policy and options even as they were primarily motivated to improve the credibility of U.S. deterrence as the threats to U.S. and allied core interests evolved. In the fourth chapter the study will focus on the inflection points in nuclear strategy, beginning in earnest with the Nixon Administration and ending with a focus on President Trump's employment strategy. The chapter will then show how the arguments modern nuclear disarmament advocates make against U.S. nuclear deterrence policy and strategy run counter to more than 50 years of U.S. nuclear deterrence policy. Adopting the disarmament views and opposing the assumptions and adaptations risks undermining the improvements U.S. strategists have made to increase the credibility of U.S. nuclear deterrence and violating JWD principles.

The study concludes by answering the question: can the United States maintain a nuclear deterrence posture that credibly meets the deterrence objectives in the modern nuclear threat environment and that is also in accordance with the JWD? The answer is a confident yes. Contrary to the views of some prominent religious leaders, improving the credibility of the U.S. nuclear deterrence posture over the years has increasingly hewed closer to the principles of the JWD. Improving the credibility of the U.S. deterrence options has led to adaptations that rightly—and with appropriate humility—seek to provide a spectrum of weapons and tools to hold at risk what the adversary values to compel the adversary to cease its attacks and return to a peace on just terms that favor the United States. Some of those adaptations include explicitly embracing a counterforce posture, improving the accuracy of weapons, maintaining the diversity of delivery systems for flexible response, maintaining a technological hedge, and investing in and deploying various active defenses.

A striking conclusion of the study is that the JWD and efforts to improve the credibility of our deterrence options *have been reinforcing and are not in conflict.* As the United States has sought to sustain the credibility of its deterrence options, it has held that the best way to do that is to have the ability to hold at risk what the adversary values most with the necessary weapons to have the desired effect. This "tailored" deterrence approach does not intentionally target opponents' society and population. The evidence shows that the Soviet Union, North Korea, the Russian Federation, or the Peoples Republic of China, appear to value most the survival of their regimes, the weapons necessary to protect their regimes, and their means of maintaining control over their populations.[42] Attempting to establish a U.S. nuclear deterrence strategy based on American political values, i.e., civilian society and population, runs an unacceptably high risk of not credibly deterring authoritarian adversaries.

For example, if the United States were to go back to threatening civilian populations, i.e., political innocents, the authoritarian adversary that does not place highest value on its general population is unlikely to be deterred reliably. Holding at risk societal targets is called "countervalue" or "counter-city."[43] Instead, U.S. deterrence strategy has sought to maintain a spectrum of options, in a variety of

---

[42] For a more in-depth discussion on what authoritarian adversaries value, see Gray, *Nuclear Strategy and Strategic Planning*, op. cit., pp. 73-74.

[43] For more on counter-value targeting, the arguments about its lack of credibility during the Cold War, and its continued lack of credibility in the current threat environment, see Keith B. Payne, *The Rejection of Intentional Population Targeting for "Tripolar" Deterrence, Occasional Paper*, Vol. 3, No. 9 (Fairfax, VA: National Institute Press, September 2023), available at https://nipp.org/papers/the-rejection-of-intentional-population-targeting-for-tripolar-deterrence/.

contingencies, to hold at risk what the adversary regimes value — and not to target deliberately civilian populations as such. As evidenced in the unclassified 2020 U.S. nuclear employment strategy,[44] the United States to this day explicitly rejects targeting cities as not credible for deterrence purposes and in violation of the LOAC. Defenses have also contributed to the success of U.S. strategic posture and intra-war deterrence as a means of protecting innocents and limiting damage of an aggressor's attacks. The 2023 bipartisan U.S. Strategic Posture Commission came to a consensus conclusion that the United States, even as it seeks to deter both Russia and China, should maintain its deterrence strategy and to comply with the LOAC.[45]

A complementary conclusion is that many efforts to restrict deterrence options in pursuit of disarmament or while clinging to nuclear pacifism *violate* the JWD. This is because they run the serious risk of deterrence failure in a way that would leave the United States more vulnerable to adversary attack, thereby abrogating the Divine mandate of government authority, which is to protect the innocent and punish the evil behavior that harms them.[46]

An additional conclusion is really the rediscovery and affirmation of the saliency in the modern geopolitical context of theologian-strategist William O'Brien's exhortation to sufficiently weigh the value of the good of what is being defended against the potential cost of its

---

[44] U.S. Department of Defense, *2020 Report to Congress on the Nuclear Employment Strategy of the United States* (Specified in Section 491 (a) of Title 10 USC, delivered November 2020), p. 6-7, available at 21-F-0591_2020_Report_of_the_Nuclear_Employement_Strategy_of_the_Unit ed_States.pdf (whs.mil).

[45] Congressional Commission on the Strategic Posture of the United States, op. cit., p. vii.

[46] Payne and Payne, *A Just Defense*, op. cit., pp. 22-23, and 38. "Scripture teaches that government is responsible to use necessary force to defend the innocent, reward good behavior, and punish evil behavior (Romans 13: 3-5; 1 Peter 2: 13-14)."

defense.[47] The principle of proportionality during a just war cannot be evaluated, or a reasonable action decided, without carefully weighing the value of what the just warrior is defending and what he is defending against. This maxim is at the heart of ethicist and political philosopher Jean Bethke Elshtain's instruction about the nature of the Just War Doctrine as neither simply consequentialist nor deontologically rigid. Instead, Elshtain argued that the just war strategist must engage with doctrinal principles, recognizing there are actions that are inherently wrong, while *of course* weighing potential consequences of certain action or inaction and pursuing the greatest possible good (as defined by maximizing the protection of the innocent and punishing those trying to harm them).[48] The just war strategist must be concerned with the intent, but intent is not enough; he must be focused on whether his intent leads to action or inaction that is likely to result in the just outcome he so desires. This concept becomes the most apparent in the discussion of the two dimensions of the principle of proportionality in warfare.

The study will conclude with a summary of findings and recommendations, above all that it is sound judgment for the JWD to guide and bolster potential changes to improve U.S. deterrence as the United States prepares for an ominous future. The protection of the United States and its people against those who seek to harm Americans and destroy the nation is the government's Divinely assigned duty and Constitutional mandate.

Morality demands more than the sincerest desire to do good and to refrain from doing evil. Morality demands that

---

[47] William V. O'Brien, "Just War Doctrine in a Nuclear Context," *Theological Studies* (June 1, 1983), p. 199.

[48] Lubomir Martin Ondrasek, "Jean Bethke Elshtain: An Augustinian at War," *Providence Magazine*, August 11, 2017, available at https://providencemag.com/wp-content/uploads/Lubomir-Martin-Ondrasek-Jean-Bethke-Elshtain.pdf.

sincere desire to act justly and refrain from evil is met with action or inaction that to the best of the statesman's judgements has the best chances of achieving just outcomes. In the modern era, with increasingly diverse and acute threats, the best way to do that is by seeking to optimize the credibility of deterrence and by preparing for the possibility that deterrence may fail, and thereby preparing to optimally defend innocents while seeking to convince the adversary to cease his aggression on the lowest levels of violence and towards a just and lasting peace. Contrary to the popular view that the righteous path is through pacifism and disarmament, there is a moral duty to deter.

Chapter One: U.S. Warfighting Ethics and Laws Are Rooted in the Just War Doctrine

"Men who take up arms against one another in public war do not cease on this account to be moral beings, responsible to one another and to God."

— *Lieber Code*

Looking over the history of the United States, one may note some instances of ghastly war crimes and other forms of atrocities committed by U.S. forces. But from the Republic's earliest days, presidents and military leaders sought to uphold a standard of right conduct in war and to hold accountable the soldier who would violate it. Against that standard, the violations stand out, grieve and anger those who expect more of the American warfighter. The 1863 General Orders Number 100 was drafted by Professor Francis Lieber and signed into law by President Abraham Lincoln.[49] In it, the United States established what is commonly believed to be the earliest official iteration of a codification of American right conduct in war, and which would grow into the laws of war. Article 15, Section 1, of the Lieber Code says, "…Men who take up arms against one another in public war do not cease on this account to be moral beings, responsible to one another and to God."

For the purposes of the scope of this study, and to keep the analysis applicable to the U.S. nuclear deterrence posture, the focus will be on contemporary military teaching on ethics in warfighting found in the Department of Defense *Law of War Manual*[50] as well as in presidential

---

[49] Abraham Lincoln, *General Orders No. 100: The Lieber Code: Instructions for the Government of Armies of the United States in the Field*, War Department, Washington, D.C., 1863, available at https://avalon.law.yale.edu/19th_century/lieber.asp.

[50] U.S. Department of Defense, *Law of War Manual* (Washington, D.C.: DoD Office of General Counsel, June 2015 (updated December 2016), p. 26.

memoranda and other official statements of national policies. The lack of exploration of the rich development of the laws of war in American history should not be interpreted as indicative of a failure to appreciate its nuances or impact on decisions to go to war and how to prosecute them. To the contrary, it is critically important to appreciate that the United States has long held that the efforts to maintain proper conduct in war and that justice and righteousness is not suspended even in matters of government-sanctioned violence and the fog of war. And, importantly, the American view of just conduct in war is based on the JWD.

The Department of Defense's *Law of War Manual* appeals directly to the JWD and even to the reasons underlying the Just War principles. It explains that, consistent with the JWD, the law of war has been categorized into *jus ad bellum* (law concerning the resort to force) and *jus in bello* (law concerning conduct during war), although the *Law of War Manual* goes on to clarify that it focuses on *jus in bello*.[51]

Chapter Two will explore the provenance, principles, and the general manner that the JWD should be used as a guide. The *Law of War Manual* effectively operationalizes the JWD so the warfighter has training and greater clarity about the lawful and ethical guidance as a representative of the U.S. military. The 2016 *Law of War Manual*, updated again in June 2023,[52] included amendments, which the Department of Defense announced were for the purpose of guarding against excessive force. The Department of Defense General Counsel Jennifer O'Connor said of the amendments,

---

[51] Ibid., p. 39.

[52] U.S. Department of Defense, "The Department of Defense Updates Its Law of War Manual," July 31, 2023, available at Defense Department Updates Its Law of War Manual > U.S. Department of Defense > Release.

"Protecting civilians in armed conflict is critical, and it's important that our legal guidance is clear and practical."[53]

The foreword of the Department of Defense's comprehensive *Law of War Manual* highlights notable moments in history wherein America sought to apply just principles during times of war. It says, "After World War II, U.S. military lawyers, trying thousands of defendants before military commissions did, in the words of Justice Robert Jackson, "Stay the hand of vengeance and voluntarily submit their captive enemies to the judgment of law" in "one of the most significant tributes that Power has ever paid to Reason." Reflecting on this distinctive history, one Chairman of the Joint Chiefs of Staff observed that "[t]he laws of war have a peculiarly American cast."[54]

The Department of Defense *Law of War Manual* instructs all military personnel in its guidance and application for U.S. treaties and its application in customary international law. Although the *Law of War Manual* was produced by the Department of Defense for the U.S. military, its authors accepted input for the most recent adaptation from military officers in ally nations including the United Kingdom, Australia, New Zealand, and Canada, which shows its broad appeal to nations of the West generally.[55]

Notably, the United States is not unique in its efforts to align with the laws of war. Positive international law also appeals to the laws of war and in doing so, the JWD. For example, it has been incorporated into the Responsibility to

---

[53] "The Department of Defense Announces Update to the Law of War Manual," *Defense.gov*, December 13, 2016, available at https://www.defense.gov/News/Releases/Release/Article/1028900/t he-department-of-defense-announces-update-to-the-law-of-war-manual/

[54] DOD, *Law of War Manual* (updated December 2016), op. cit., p. ii.

[55] Ibid., p. v.

Protect and the Geneva Conventions.[56] The 1977 Geneva Protocol I explicitly outlines one of the principles of the JWD, that of discrimination between combatants and noncombatants.[57] This points to the abiding relevance of the JWD even, and especially, in the atomic age.

---

[56] Keith Gomes, "An Intellectual Genealogy of the Just War: A Survey of Christian Political Thought on the Justification of Warfare," *Small Wars Journal* (August 2008), available at https://smallwarsjournal.com/blog/journal/docs-temp/80-gomes.pdf.

[57] William V. O'Brien, *The Conduct of Just and Limited War,* op. cit., p. 49.

Chapter Two: The Just War Doctrine and Its Provenance, Purpose, and Principles

"I do not believe your laws, you being only a man, sufficient to overrule divine ordinances — unwritten and unfailing as they are."

— Antigone[58]

Before focusing more closely on the JWD, it is important to situate those who embrace the JWD clearly in the proper conceptual framework within the discipline of international relations. Within the discipline, there are two schools of thought based on different assumptions that portend various and frequently conflicting policy recommendations. In 1962, renowned and quintessential realist Hans Morgenthau observed that "the history of modern political thought is the story of a contest between two schools that differ fundamentally in their conceptions of the nature of man, society, and politics."[59] The two schools of thought are realism and idealism.

The idealist believes it is both possible and necessary to strive towards permanent global solutions that make conflict and outright war among nations a thing of the past. Often that means idealists aim for multinational or transnational global institutions, seeking the ultimate global governance that arbitrates disagreements among nations and enforces international rules. In this vision, national leaders willingly set aside national preferences, short-term prosperity, and even national power and sovereignty for the sake of a greater good based on the goal of universal wellbeing.

---

[58] Quoted in Tom Holland, *Dominion: How the Christian Revolution Remade the World*, Basic Books, New York, 2019, p. 35.

[59] Quoted in Keith B. Payne, "Realism, Idealism, Deterrence, and Disarmament," op. cit., p. 7.

The League of Nations, established in 1920 at the close of the first world war to keep world peace, is the quintessential example of an attempt at the idealist vision. Jane Addams, a well-known peace activist of the period, promoted the League of Nations as more than a practical and pragmatic solution to challenges. Peace activists at the time regarded the League in salvific terms. When President Wilson was promoting the League and suffered a stroke, promoters of the League described him as a martyr.[60] But surrendering one's national defense in favor of an international entity's arbitration requires all nations to comply equally. And neither Germany's Adolf Hitler nor Imperial Japan's Hirohito shared the idealist vision.

Nations' conflicting national interests, their systems of government, the ideological motivations of their leaders and people, and security threats, persist in motivating nations to build armies. For the world's nations to forgo their nuclear weapons in favor of a global international arbiter and disarmament, all nuclear nations would have to surrender their arsenals simultaneously and trust the global institution for protection. For if even one nation retained nuclear weapons, no other nuclear weapons state would likely surrender its weapons out of fear of the one. The United Nations is the League's equally ineffective offspring. But just because global disarmament has not yet happened, the idealist persists in the belief that it is still possible.[61]

The idealist sees mounting evidence of, and the need for, this global transition all around him: he perceives existential crises facing the planet and the objectively rational thing, to the idealist's mind, is to lay down one's

---

[60] Jean Bethke Elshtain, "Peace, Order, Justice: Competing Understandings," *Millennium Journal of International Studies*, Vol. 36, No. 3 (2008), p. 419.

[61] See, for example Ronald J. Sider and Richard K Taylor, *Nuclear Holocaust and Christian Hope: A Book for Christian Peacemakers* (Downers Grove, IL: Intervarsity Press, 1982), chapter 12.

arms (starting with the nuclear ones) and submit one's power and national sovereignty to serve the wellbeing of the human family.[62] Idealists believe that there are ample reasons for rational people of good will to want and work toward global governance. They see impending climate catastrophe, nuclear holocaust, virulent viral plagues, or poverty and misery because of vast global economic inequity, and believe that all enlightened people of good will demand cooperation and progress towards global solutions. And even if the "global community" is not quite there yet, for the idealist, the world is marching, evolving, towards that goal.

Idealists embrace the assumption that since human beings are rational actors, with enough education and in light of the global existential crises, or social engineering, human beings will eventually assent to the international governing body's rationale and comply with its plan. Once global governance is in place, idealists are confident that there would no longer be a need for nuclear weapons and full disarmament would not only be acceptable but imperative. Notably, the idealist's logic never explains why national leaders should expect a global government to act as no nation-state government does, with perfect knowledge and clear-headed judgment, and in all altruism and benevolence.

Keith Payne responds to the idealist aspiration:

> The experience of all history, including at the national level where some particular affinities tend to help hold peoples together, is that government institutions of all varieties, once established, have engaged in such behaviors to the extreme dissatisfaction of some constituents — as is

---

[62] See, for example, Beatrice Fihn's Nobel Peace Prize Acceptance Speech, December 10, 2017, available at https://www.wagingpeace.org/beatrice-fihn-nobel-peace-prize-acceptance-speech.

demonstrated by the continuous lineage of political upheavals, rebellions, revolutions, and civil wars across the globe. Why, now, should we expect global governance not to reflect occasional or frequent errors of inconsistency, aggression, and pugnacity? Why should it be expected, that somehow, a new global body of some variety would be error-free and transcend seemingly enduring human limits? [63]

In stark contrast to the idealist framework, realists hold that states are the primary political drivers in the world, and that no national government can entirely trust in the intentions and prospective actions of others. The reality is that each state must help itself in an anarchic world disinclined towards harmony. Kenneth Waltz, the father of structural realism, explained, "Because each state is the final judge of his own cause, any state may at any time use force to implement its policies. Because any state may at any time use force, all states must constantly be ready either to counter force with force or to pay the cost of weakness. The requirements of state action are, in this view, imposed by the circumstances in which all states exist."[64] Ultimately, states are motivated to pursue power so that they can act based on their own conceptions of their security requirements and interests. [65] While allies over time can

---

[63] Keith B. Payne, *Chasing a Grand Illusion: Replacing Deterrence with Disarmament* (Fairfax, VA: National Institute Press, 2023), p. 67.

[64] Kenneth Waltz, *Man, The State, and War* (Columbia University Press, New York, 1954) p. 160.

[65] Here I use "security and perceived interests" to mean what each regime considers vital, but those motives certainly might include what the United States might consider non rational or ideologically motivated. Donald Kagan explained that the realistic and constant state in global affairs is the struggle for power. Kagan writes, "In the struggle for power, whether for a rational sufficiency or in the insatiable drive for all the power there is, Thucydides found that people go to war out

earn a measure of trust and even affection as in personal relationships, national governments prioritize their nation's own security and perceived interests above all.

For the realist, alliances are possible and treaties useful to the extent that the alliances and the treaties further the security and interests of the member nations as they see them. The 2022 *Nuclear Posture Review*, for example, explicitly rejected the Treaty on the Prohibition of Nuclear Weapons (TPNW), as an effective tool for eliminating nuclear weapons because it ignored the realities of the international security environment that drive states to seek or retain nuclear weapons.[66] Likewise, the NATO Communique issued on July 11, 2023, at the NATO Summit in Vilnius, Lithuania, denounced the TPNW, staying it "stands in opposition to and is inconsistent and incompatible with the Alliance's nuclear deterrence policy."[67]

---

of 'honor, fear, and interest.'" Donald Kagan, *On the Origins of War and the Preservation of Peace* (New York, Doubleday, 1995), p. 8. This reality, of nation states vying for power, is not only a description of what is, as scholar Colin Dueck observes, "In the early modern era, European philosophers in this civic tradition [civic nationalism] argued that the world was best governed by independent nation-states, precisely in order to protect the freedoms of both countries and individuals. The belief was that every nation had its own traditions worth preserving — and that only within the context of a sovereign nation-state could individual citizens experiment with versions of republican or constitutional rule. This belief eventual had immense impact worldwide, helping to reorder the international system along lines of national sovereignty and self-determination." Colin Dueck, *Age of Iron* (New York, Oxford University Press, 2009) p. 9.

[66] U.S. Department of Defense, *Nuclear Posture Review* (Washington, D.C.: Department of Defense, 2022), p.19, available at https://media.defense.gov/2022/Oct/27/2003103845/-1/-1/1/2022-NATIONAL-DEFENSE-STRATEGY-NPR-MDR.PDF.

[67] North Atlantic Treaty Organization, Vilnius Summit Communique, (Vilnius, Lithuania, North Atlantic Council, July 11, 2023), available at NATO - Official text: Vilnius Summit Communiqué issued by NATO Heads of State and Government (2023), 11-Jul.-2023.

Realists are highly skeptical that human efforts can secure the idealists' global transition and achieve a permanent peace because the structure of the international system compels states to seek power to preserve their security and the goals between state will conflict. A reliably peaceful global system, or anything resembling it, is unreachable short of an unprecedented and unknown event or divine intervention.[68] Instead, realists see history as moving down a timeline wherein peace, conflict, and war come and go. The task for the realist policymaker is to take a humbler approach and maximize his country's advantages and security as best as he can, within the limits of what is humanly practicable, in the short time he has the power to do so.

Scholarship and commentary related to international relations often make the mistake of ascribing notions about morality and national principles or "values" and human rights necessarily only to the idealist school of thought. And a corollary to this mistake is the erroneous idea that those who are realists believe that only state security and power balances among nations are predictive of behavior and that notions about ideology or systems of government are nothing more than smokescreens for pure power politics or realpolitik.[69] But some realists believe that, of course one

---

[68] In Mark Tooley, "Christian Realism vs. Christian Nationalism," *Providence Magazine*, September 8, 2022, available at Christian Realism vs Christian Nationalism - Providence (providencemag.com) the contemporary Protestant Christian Realist scholar explains, "For Christian Realism, there is no idealized past, nor is there an idealized future, short of the eschaton. Instead, in our fallen circumstances, we seek to follow God by seeking the greatest good possible in constrained situations, understanding that we ourselves lack absolute wisdom."

[69] In Donald Kagan, "On the Origins of War and the Preservation of Peace," op. cit., pp. 7-8, Kagan differentiates between the realists who posit that all political leaders seek power for its own sake while neorealists seek power for the preservation of security and other goods. Kagan assesses that both brands of realism lack a fuller understanding

must account for the subjective complex motives of state leaders including regime ideology, risk tolerance, strategic cultures, as well as assessments of adversary nations' political wills, risk tolerances, economic wherewithal, and military capabilities.[70]

Reality, War, and Morality

Having established two different frameworks within the discipline of international relations, it will become clear that the JWD is predicated on the assumptions that support the realist framework for understanding and seeking to navigate international affairs. Nuclear strategist and practitioner Keith Payne, and his brother, pastor and theologian Karl Payne, explain that this anthropological reality of man's fallenness and the related anarchic structure of international relations are the root cause of the inherent mistrust among nation-states in the international system.[71] This fallenness is the Christian view of man's rebellion against God's perfect knowledge and standard of justice and righteousness. The broad and ecumenical view of Christians is that man is capable of great good due to the

---

of the motivations of war, and points to the fifth century historian, Thucydides, who concluded that people go to war our of "honor, fear, and interest."

[70] For a discussion on the way regimes and cultures impact deterrence see Colin S. Gray, *Nuclear Strategy and Strategic Planning,* op. cit., pp. 61-67. See also Etel Solingen, "Nuclear Logics: Contrasting Paths in East Asia and the Middle East," (United Kingdom: Princeton University Press, 2007), for a closer examination of the shortcomings of prominent models that strategists often use to explain or predict possible nuclear behavior, and an assessment of the importance of considering the impact of domestic politics, systems of government, and regime leaders on the nuclear behaviors of various nations.

[71] For a discussion on the root cause of the chaotic international system, especially as a refutation to the idealist aim of global government, see Keith B. Payne and Karl I. Payne, *A Just Defense,* op. cit., pp. 153-167. See also Kenneth Waltz, *Man, The State, and War,* op. cit., pp. 159-186.

doctrine of *Imago Dei* (Genesis 1:27),[72] but is limited in knowledge and often acts according to his own aggrandizement. The traditional Christian doctrine of original sin holds that most men do not even try to follow God's objective and eternal standard of righteousness, and those who do by Divine grace, are incapable of doing good without error.[73] Although over time there has been human progress in some aspects, Christian teaching holds that the world's brokenness and man's fallenness will persist until God's intervention and final act in the Christian view of the biblical arc of redemption. Augustinian scholars describe mankind's state as undergoing changes but reject the progressivist view of continual transformation towards the ideal.[74] And so, just as human fallibility is a constant throughout human history, conflict and war among nations has been, too. But for the just warrior striving to obey God's will for mankind, war is not the preferred solution to disputes between nations.

The Christian realist (or if one accepts the JWD precepts embraced by Christianity but employs natural law and reason as the basis, he may describe himself as a "moral realist") prefers that violence is not the *modus operandi* for dealing with disputes to save or return to peace. Instead, these realists strive for peace by resolving disputes diplomatically if possible, and by seeking to convince other nations not to pursue actions that would threaten the security of the political innocents he is responsible for: that is, his fellow citizens. But while the just warrior prefers non-

---

[72] Genesis 1:27, "So God created man in his own image, in the image of God he created him male and female he created them." English Standard Version.

[73] In Romans 7:15 the Apostle Paul expresses and laments the reality of the Christian state, "For I do not understand my own actions. For I do not do what I want, but I do the very thing I hate."

[74] For a more in-depth treatment of this matter, please see Jean Bethke Elshtain, *Augustine and the Limits of Politics*, op. cit., Chapter 5.

violent means for solving disputes, he has fixed in his mind that peace is not the highest aim. One only need look across the globe to see that there are leaders who seek to enslave, destroy, or otherwise coerce citizens of other sovereign nations to surrender their rights. If peace is the highest aim, in the face of aggression, surrender is the obvious choice; but surrender may doom the innocent. For the Christian realist, the Holy Scriptures mandate that justice sometimes requires forceful defense of the innocent.

For the just warrior, peace at the price of surrender could come at the cost of liberty, prosperity, self-determination, and the lives and wellbeing of innocent people. That peace comes at too high a cost and paying it would entail the renunciation of the Christian's view of the fundamental Divinely appointed reason for government: the protection of the innocent everywhere and punishment of an adversary who would do them harm. Consequently, to fulfill the government's Divine duty, the threat or use of force and war are not always avoidable.

The biblical basis for this Christian belief is rooted in the Book of Romans. The Apostle of Jesus, Paul, exhorts:

> Let every person be subject to the governing authorities. For there is no authority except from God, and those that exist have been instituted by God. [2] Therefore whoever resists the authorities resists what God has appointed, and those who resist will incur judgment. [3] For rulers are not a terror to good conduct, but to bad. Would you have no fear of the one who is in authority? Then do what is good, and you will receive his approval, [4] for he is God's servant for your good. But if you do wrong, be afraid, for he does not bear the sword in vain. For he is the servant of God, an avenger who carries out God's wrath on the wrongdoer. [5] Therefore one must be in subjection, not only to avoid God's wrath but also for the sake

of conscience. [6] For because of this you also pay taxes, for the authorities are ministers of God, attending to this very thing. [7] Pay to all what is owed to them: taxes to whom taxes are owed, revenue to whom revenue is owed, respect to whom respect is owed, honor to whom honor is owed.[75]

Keith and Karl Payne exposit the main points that Christians who embrace the JWD look to for guidance. God institutes government and the role and authority of government is specific, limited, accountable to God's judgment,[76] and different than that of the private citizen.[77] And the use of force or "bearing the sword" is for the government to do good for the citizens under its care, to protect them, and to punish those who would harm them.[78]

---

[75] Romans 13: 1-7, English Standard Version.

[76] A common view of the Scriptures held by Christians is that all government authority is instituted by God but that does not grant government license to do as it pleases without regard to God's standard of justice. As theology scholar and Baptist Pastor Jonathan Leeman writes in Jonathan Leeman, *The Political Church: The Local Assembly as Embassy of Christ's Rule* (Downers Grove, Illinois: IVP, 2016), p. 196; "[W]e only need observe that no government should presume to be above the justice mechanism, but government must always remain under it (1) because the authority ultimately derives from God an (2) because every member of society is created in God's image. As such, every government is subject to the demands of the justice mechanism."

[77] Keith and Karl Payne point to other critical Scriptures that show why JW Christian scholars view that simply because God institutes government, it does not therefore mean that earthly government is unable to error or that the Christian must obey the government when it usurps authority from God, especially pointing to Matthew 22:21 when Christ instructs "Give to Caesar what is Caesar's, and to God what is God's." Payne and Payne, *A Just Defense*, op. cit., p. 25.

[78] Ibid., pp. 22-23, and 38. Note also that "Scripture teaches that government is responsible to use necessary force to defend the innocent, reward good behavior, and punish evil behavior (Romans 13: 3-5; 1 Peter 2: 13-14)."

So, what is the highest aim for the citizen concerned about morality if not only peace? The aim of a just war is peace with justice.[79] The maxim that peace in accordance with justice, as manifested at least in part by the protection of the good and political innocent, is the highest aim has led to a pressing and urgent question that theologians and statesmen have sought to answer and that was the genesis of the JWD. Since distrust among nations is perennial and conflict predictable, and peace through diplomatic and economic means and even elusive, is it possible for the person who prizes justice and protection, based on Biblical precepts, to support a nation entering and fighting a war? Can the pious Christian engage in warfare in defense of his nation? It is by asking these questions, and looking to the Holy Scriptures and reason, that men and women developed the JWD and in doing so placed both limits and duties on the just government and warrior.

President Barack Obama provided a summary of the motivation and formation of the Just War Doctrine when he accepted the Nobel Peace Prize in 2009 for his aspirations towards nuclear disarmament. He said:

> And over time, as codes of law sought to control violence within groups, so did philosophers and clerics and statesmen seek to regulate the destructive power of war. The concept of a just war emerged, suggesting that war is justified only when certain conditions were met: if it is waged as a last resort or in self-defense; if the force used is proportional; and if, whenever possible, civilians are spared from violence.[80]

---

[79] Ibid., p. 46.

[80] President Barack Obama, "Remarks by the President at the Acceptance of the Nobel Peace Prize," *Whitehouse.gov,* December 10, 2009, available at https://obamawhitehouse.archives.gov/the-press-office/remarks-president-acceptance-nobel-peace-prize.

President Obama's Administration, however committed to the disarmament agenda, remained committed to deterrence. It would go on to maintain the nuclear triad, eschew altering the U.S. nuclear declaratory policy, invest in nuclear modernization, and would indeed keep and affirm U.S. nuclear doctrine and its compatibility with JWD principles.

The scholars and theologians who contributed the most to the tapestry of the JWD did so because they understood the reality of distrust among nations, the persistent condition of man's fallenness, and the perennial conflict that would arise due to that mistrust and fallenness. Given these realities, they anticipate no basis for the idealist aspiration of man establishing a benevolent, global government and abolishing war. To add to the Madisonian axiom in Federalist 51, "If men were angels, no government would be necessary"[81]… and there would be no need for the JWD.[82]

The renowned Georgetown University professor and political philosopher William O'Brien reviews the assumptions of the JWD and points out, as is posited here, that the just warrior begins with a theological presumption against war as the preferred choice for dealing with disputes. This harkens back to the Roman jurist Cicero (106 BC- 46 BC) who sought to articulate the framework for waging a just war. He instructed that "war should be undertaken in such a way that it may seem nothing else than a quest for peace. … Yet when occasion and need demand, there must be hand-to-hand fighting, and death is to be

---

[81] James Madison, The Federalist Papers, No. 51, New York, NY, February 8, 1788, available at https://avalon.law.yale.edu/18th_century/fed51.asp.

[82] This point is inspired by and supported by the views expressed by John W. Coffey in "Deterrence and the Bishops: A Trans-Atlantic Comparison," *Strategic Review*, Vol. 14, No. 1 (Winter 1986), p. 66.

preferred to slavery and poltroonery."[83] As explained by O'Brien, for the defense of the innocent and public order, a just government can and sometimes must overcome the presumption against war.[84] The JWD principles are designed to help policymakers and soldiers navigate a world comprised of diverse and distrustful nations that is tumultuous, perennially challenging, and often violent in pursuit of hostile aims. Although it is exceedingly challenging and requires constant intellectual effort and examination, for the just warrior: "Peace *with justice* is the goal of a just war,"[85] or at least as proximate as one can be in this imperfect world. In a compelling Cold War-era essay on Christian morality and nuclear deterrence, Captain Charles Nicholls says the JWD "should be cherished as an attempt to limit that evil, not as a standard of absolute morality."[86]

By asking the questions when and how one might rightfully engage in warfare, scholars have agreed on broad principles. The result of this body of scholarly work is best understood, to use the word employed by Donald L. Davidson, as an "amalgamation" of Western thought. This amalgamation is the JWD. [87] Although the JWD does not provide a precise proscription for how to respond to nations that challenge the just defending nation, it does offer the most "relevant principles that are intelligible, generalizable,

---

[83] Marcus Tullius Cicero, *On Duties*, translated by Andrew P. Peabody (Salt Lake City, UT: Stonewell Press, 2013) p. 29.

[84] William V. O'Brien, "Just War Doctrine in a Nuclear Context," op. cit., p. 192.

[85] Payne and Payne, *A Just Defense*, op. cit., p. 46 (emphasis added).

[86] Charles Nichols, "Christian Morality and Nuclear Deterrence," *Air University Review* (July/August 1985), p. 39.

[87] As quoted in Donald Davidson, *Nuclear Weapons and the American Churches: Ethical Positions on Modern Warfare* (Boulder, CO: Westview Press, 1983), p. 1.

and capable of consistent application," according to Presbyterian pastor and prominent ethicist Ralph Potter.[88]

The JWD begins with the view that human life is of great value and that the taking of human life is serious and carries with it significant moral implications, and therefore demands careful consideration. JWD holds that murder is the *unjust* killing of human beings and is never permissible. But taking of human life is not necessarily murder; it can be permissible if it done under proper authority and conforms to the principles of justice.[89] Thus, taking human life can be carried out justly, but it is fraught with challenges and difficulties, and so the JWD seeks to provide guidance for practitioners in matters of war, but it recognizes that war ought to be avoided if possible rather than the preferential modus operandi for dealing with disputes among nations.[90] Karl Barth instructs: "It is no part of the normal task of the state to wage war; its normal task is to fashion peace in such a way that life is served and war kept at bay. It is when the state does not rightly pursue its normal task that sooner or later it is compelled to take up the abnormal one of war, and therefore to inflict this abnormal task on other states."[91]

Building on the work of the Greeks and Romans, scholarship considering the morality of war was further developed by giants in the Catholic Church, Ambrose of Milan (339-397 AD) and Augustine of Hippo (354-430 AD) and then famously Thomas Aquinas (1225-1274), who blends natural law tradition with biblical ethics. In Aquinas's most important work, *Summa Theologica*, he sets out both *in bello* and *ad bellum* criteria grounded in Christian

---

[88] Ibid., p. 14.

[89] Ibid., p. 19.

[90] Keith Gomes, "An Intellectual Genealogy of the Just War: A Survey of Christian Political Thought on the Justification of Warfare," *Small Wars Journal* (August 2008), p. 2.

[91] Quoted in Paul Ramsey, *The Just War: Force and Political Responsibility*, (New York: Charles Scribner's Sons, 1966), p. 5.

ethics.[92] For them, the just warrior must intend to do good and avoid evil and also match his actions with his intent for outcomes that advance justice. Aquinas helpfully illustrates what the just warrior does not seek to do, "What is evil in war? … The desire for harming, the cruelty of avenging, an unruly and implacable animosity, the rage of rebellion, the lust of domination and the like."[93]

O'Brien instructs that a helpful way to consider Aquinas's teaching on just war is that he (and the Scholastics) dealt with the morality of war in terms of "grace-elevated natural law." This means that Aquinas and those who held to his views on JWD could draw from the entirety of the biblical account of human history and future, and of Christ's teaching about the fallenness of human nature.[94] Although Catholic social teaching on JWD has contributed mightily to the JWD, it is not a uniquely or even primarily a Catholic view within the Christian tradition.

Paul Ramsey, preeminent JWD scholar, points to prominent Christian Confessions including the Augsburg and Westminster, which embrace the possibility of engaging in war justly and the duty to do so.[95] Ramsey says that Martin Luther and John Calvin in the 16th century embraced robust theories of statecraft that overlapped with, were compatible with, and built on Catholic JWD teaching, even if they also dissented in some key areas.[96]

For example, Martin Luther held that wars are necessary to right wrongs and maximize the defense of the innocent in a world of injustice and unjust peace, and soldiers are as "useful to the world as eating or drinking or any other

---

[92] Gomes, *An Intellectual Genealogy of the Just War*, op. cit., p. 9.

[93] Marc LiVecche, *The Good Kill: Just War and Moral Injury*, (Oxford, UK: Oxford University Press, 2021), p. 91.

[94] William V. O'Brien, *The Conduct of Just and Limited War,* op. cit., p. 15.

[95] Ramsey, *The Just War,* op. cit., p. xii.

[96] Ibid., p. xiii.

work."[97] Likewise, John Calvin said that in addition to a just cause, right intent and the principle of last resort are moral imperatives: "the evident object of war ought to be the restoration of peace, and certainly we ought to make every other attempt before we have recourse to the decision of arms."[98]

Ramsey famously fleshed out the meaning of the Christian's view of the Biblical command to love one's neighbor in the context of certain kinds of violence. War is justified, according to Ramsay, when the motive is to protect the innocent against the "bearer of hostile force." And then the just warrior must seek to wage the war justly out of the same motivation.[99] For Ramsay, the strain of pacifist thought in the Christian tradition fails to meet the criteria for justice: "The Christian is commanded to do anything a realistic love commands (and so sometimes he must fight)."[100]

As previously discussed, prominent JWD scholars derive their assumptions about justice and government from the Holy Scriptures, taking the Old and New Testaments together. To reiterate, JWD Christian scholars hold the view that God instituted government for good purposes.[101] According to their exegesis of the Holy Scriptures, the governing authorities "bear the sword,"[102] that is, they have the divinely appointed duty to coerce, and to use force, if necessary, for the purpose of maintaining order, punishing evil, protecting the innocent, and if there

---

[97] Quoted in Keith Gomes, *An Intellectual Genealogy,* op. cit., p. 17.

[98] Ibid., p. 11.

[99] Ramsey, *The Just War,* op. cit., p. 143.

[100] Ibid., p. 145.

[101] For an especially profound Biblical exhortation to recognize that all authority comes from God and God alone, see John 19:10-11, quoted in Payne and Payne, *A Just Defense,* op. cit., p. 26.

[102] Editorial Staff, "A Proposal to Tilt the Balance of Terror," *Christianity Today,* April 9, 1982, p. 17.

is a breakdown of just peace, restoring a just peace (see Romans 13: 1-7, 1 Peter 2: 13-14).[103] It is fundamental for the purposes of this study to establish that JWD theologians and scholars, drawing from Biblical precepts, recognize a difference between a government's divine mandate and the private religious institutions and the citizen's duties.[104] Even if some Christians choose pacifism in their private capacity as a civilian according to the dictates of their consciences, the JWD does not permit such a choice for governments. The JWD is derived from the belief that governments are instituted by God for the mandates listed above. Those mandates sometimes *require* the government and its representatives to exercise the coercive and violent use of "the sword" or military force, and by abstaining from using force when necessary, the government is in violation of its divine mandate and could even be complicit in the evil that it refuses to stop.

A prominent clerical leader in the Catholic Church, James Schall, reminds:

> [T]he Church has always adhered to the necessity of protecting the innocent against brutality and oppression, combatting injustice, and defending justice and righteousness. As we know from the lessons of history, a universal renunciation of this

---

[103] Payne and Payne, *A Just Defense*, op. cit., p. 42.

[104] The student of political philosophy will be unsatisfied with the study's shallow attention provided to this subject, which is a deep well and deserving of a treatise all its own. For more on this subject, please see Leeman, *Political Church*, op. cit. p. 73. Leeman helpfully establishes this "two-kingdoms" paradigm within the Protestant (Martin Luther) and especially American Founding historical landscape. Leeman notes that "[John] Locke argued that governments should concern themselves with the 'outward things' such as 'life, liberty, health, and the indolency of body' as well as 'the money, lands, houses, and furniture, and the like.' He offered this as a point in contrast with the church whose jurisdiction he said lies with the 'care of the souls' and the 'inward and full persuasion of the mind.'"

protection and resistance may be understood as weakness and possibly as an invitation to perpetuate political blackmail.[105]

But not all prominent JWD writers proceed from a strictly Christian perspective. One of the most famous and influential scholars is Dutch jurist Hugo Grotius (1583-1645).[106] Grotius argued that justice in war was necessary and knowable apart from Biblical texts and could be discerned through natural law. His works were taught in the prominent Leiden University and imported to the new American Republic. Grotius is known as the father of international law and to underscore his impact on the American way of thinking, there is a bas-relief of his portrait alongside Moses, Hammurabi, and Thomas Jefferson in the U.S. House of Representatives.[107]

In *A Just Defense*, Karl and Keith Payne cite Dr. Robert Culver's summary of what has been a broad appeal of just war thinking. He said:

> Nature has endowed man with a desire for peace and order and with the power of reason that makes possible an ordered society. True law is right reason in accordance with nature. It is unchanging and universal. It summons us to duty even to our enemies; it precludes treachery; it requires that even war be governed by moral law.[108]

After having established the purpose and origins of the JWD, this study examines what this theological and

---

[105] James Schall, ed., S.J., *Out of Justice, Peace: Joint Pastoral Letter of the West German Bishops,* and *Winning the Peace: Joint Pastoral Letter of the French Bishops* (San Francisco, CA: Ignatius Press, 1984), p. 68.

[106] Ibid., p. 13.

[107] Russell Shorto, *The Island at the Center of the World* (New York: Vintage Books, 2005) p. 99.

[108] Payne and Payne, *A Just Defense,* op. cit., p. 44.

philosophical scholarship wrought that so amazingly established common ground across Catholicism, Protestantism, and those who argued strictly from natural law.

Taxonomy of Just War

The JWD has two categories: *jus ad bellum* (law concerning the [decision to] resort to force) and *jus in bello* (law concerning conduct during war). In the first category, the principles are as follows: just cause, the "premier criterion,"[109] sovereign authority; formal declaration; proportionality (meaning, the anticipated destruction cannot be greater than what it seeks to save/prevent);[110] right intention, which must always have as the objective of a "just and lasting peace"[111] and cannot be, as St. Augustine warned against, for greed, cruelty, or revenge;[112] last resort; and probability of success. Probability of success is tied to the principle of intention, the seeking of a just and lasting peace.

In the second category, *jus in bello*, i.e., conduct during war, the principles are proportionality (which includes the principle of right intention to defend the innocent and a restoration of a just and lasting peace)[113] and discrimination, which means that since noncombatants are political

---

[109] Davidson, *Nuclear Weapons and the American Churches*, op. cit., p. 24.

[110] Ibid., p. 30.

[111] O'Brien, *The Conduct of Just and Limited War*, op. cit., p. 34.

[112] Ibid., p. 34.

[113] In James Turner Johnson, *Can Modern War Be Just?* (New Haven, CT: Yale University Press, 1984), p. 89, the author cites John Locke's inveighing against "scorched earth policy," which echoed Deuteronomy 20:19-20. This Scripture warned against cutting down fruit trees and vineyards in warfare.

innocents they must not be intentionally targeted.[114] The two principles are symbiotically related. While it is never morally acceptable to intentionally target civilians in warfare, the realist understands that it is not possible to know with certainty that there will be zero civilian casualties even if the just warrior seeks to avoid them. In a limited non-nuclear war, there are unintended and lamented civilian casualties. While certain categories of weapons with larger potential explosive effects may pose a greater risk of civilian casualties, they may need to be employed to destroy a specific military locale or capability critical to countering an aggressor's campaign of violence and thereby protecting the innocent. And so, the just warrior must judicially choose the appropriate weapon and employment to achieve the needed military and political effects, while trying to avoid and not intentionally harming the political innocents on or near to the battlefield.

The principle of proportionality can only be understood in view of the realities of the JWD's principle of discrimination. According to the JWD, proportionality requires that the potential unintended harm to innocents be acceptable only when compared to the desired military aim; the military aim must seek to limit the possible unintended harm to non-combatants in a warrior's campaign to fight his enemy in pursuit of the defense of the innocent. Proportionality also seeks to guard against any temptation to vengeance and cruelty against one's enemy and civilians sympathetic to one's enemy.

This principle of proportionality provides guidance in those cases where some violation of non-combatant immunity is possible but unintended. In other words, the just warrior may realize that a military act of violence he

---

[114] Ibid., p. 28, where Johnson wrote, "Warfare in which combatants and noncombatants are perceived and treated as essentially alike is fundamentally against the major moral tradition of war in Western culture."

believes necessary to achieving the just military aim may entail unintended harm to political innocents. In this scenario, the military action is morally acceptable only if the value of the action with the right intention of the *defense of the innocent* and restoration of peace on just terms is so great that the unintentional and undesired violation of the non-combatant immunity can be accepted even if lamented — with a clear conscience. Put another way, the possibility of inflicting a measure of unintended harm against some innocents may be acceptable, if using that level of military force is critical and proportional to achieving the moral goal — indeed, in such a scenario military action is morally required.[115]

The consideration of proportionality in warfare helpfully illustrates the merits of the JWD and guards against improper uses or unrealistic expectations of it. The JWD identifies moral strictures and rejects utilitarianism and pure consequentialism without, as Jean Bethke Elshtain admonished, applying "deontological rigidities."[116] Deontology is concerned with the action itself, regardless of the consequence. The JWD gives no license to inherently wrong actions even if they bring good. Neither does it only value the good intention of the scholar or policymaker. The just warrior may be well intentioned, but he must be judged in part on what his just intentions require him to do and then what those actions (or inactions) yield. The aim is to have the right intent, the right outcome, and the good of the consequence of his decisive action or inaction. Niebuhr noted: "In statecraft, consequentialist considerations must be part of the calculus, for policymakers cannot afford purely abstract deontological reasoning, but rather must

---

[115] William V. O'Brien, "A Just War Deterrence/Defense Strategy," *Center Journal* (Winter 1983), p. 17.

[116] Lubomir Martin Ondrasek, "Jean Bethke Elshtain: An Augustinian at War," *Providence Magazine*, August 11, 2017, available at Jean Bethke Elshtain: An Augustinian at War - Providence (providencemag.com).

root their policy choices in realities of a morally broken world in which we all live."[117]

Building on Niebuhr's observation, it is nonsensical to seek to use the just war principles for warfare in the hopes of perfect outcomes since those principles have been considered and expounded precisely because the world is not a utopia in which perfect outcomes realistically may be demanded or anticipated. This is true in conventional war and the U.S. military is trained to carry out its missions as proximate to these just aims as possible. There is not an exception for weapons required for larger scale war. And the same is just as true when it comes to nuclear deterrence and strategic planning. The aim of the JWD is to equip the policymaker to align his actions as closely as possible to justice. To do this, he must consider the principles of discrimination and proportionality by weighing the just cause of the act of violence with the cost of defending it. There will be a cost—that is not in question. But it is not moral for a government to refuse to defend a righteous cause in protection of the innocent against a repressive aggressor that is intending to do grave harm and injustice because the perfect employment of force and outcome are not possible.

Instead, as O'Brien reasons, "[J]ust war doctrine requires a calculation of proportionality between the just cause and the cost of its defense. How such a calculation can be attempted without an evaluation of the just cause, the referent of proportionality, is beyond my understanding."[118] This rings especially true in the atomic age, and in the contemporary threat environment with two ambitious authoritarian powers bent on replacing the United States as the world's preeminent power and instead

---

[117] Mark Tooley, review of *Niebuhrian International Relations*, by Gregory J. Moore, *Law and Liberty*, June 23, 2021, available at https://lawliberty.org/book-review/niebuhrs-christian-realism.

[118] O'Brien, "Just War Doctrine in a Nuclear Context," op. cit., p. 199.

shaping the order and global dynamics to benefit their respective authoritarian regimes at the expense of U.S. security, freedom, and prosperity. The stakes are great—the just cause is to protect Americans, our allies, and liberty against authoritarian nations and their violent and totalitarian designs. The principle of proportionality, especially for the mission of deterring nuclear attack, requires the just warrior to keep the just cause and just actions fixed in his mind.

Chapter Three: Idealism, Nuclear Disarmament, and Nuclear Pacifism

"The problem lies not in the weapons, but in the nature of humankind."

— *Franklin Miller*[119]

The ranking of values is necessary in any ethic. Professor of religion James Turner Johnson illustrates this prioritization well by contrasting the way humanist Erasmus and utilitarian John Stuart Mill grapple with the question of whether war can ever be moral. For Mill, "war is an ugly thing, but not the ugliest thing."[120] There are things worse than death, such as slavery and oppression. Military weapons generally, and nuclear weapons specifically, have no intrinsic moral value. They can be threatened or employed for effects that protect innocents, limit human suffering brought by slavery and oppression, and protect freedom, self-determination, and human life. Therefore, since nuclear deterrence "has staved off the direct suicidal confrontation between superpowers" as Schall claims,[121] then James Child is correct in concluding that "[n]uclear surrender and the nuclear pacifism that mandates it is, in the most accurate definition that law and political theory

---

[119] Franklin Miller, "Disarmament and Deterrence: A Practitioner's View," Carnegie Endowment for Peace, February 13, 2009, available at chrome-extension://efaidnbmnnnibpcajpcglclefindmkaj/https://carnegieendowment.org/files/Miller1.pdf.

[120] Charles Dunlap, "Is the Treaty Banning Nuclear Weapons Immoral?," *War on the Rocks* (August 2, 2017), quoting John Stewart Mill, *Principles of Political Economy* (1881), article available at https://warontherocks.com/2017/08/is-the-treaty-banning-nuclear-weapons-immoral.

[121] James Schall, ed., S.J., *Out of Justice, Peace: Joint Pastoral Letter of the West German Bishops*, and *Winning the Peace: Joint Pastoral Letter of the French Bishops* (San Francisco, CA: Ignatius Press, 1984), p. 112.

can provide, submission to slavery, for it is submission to the arbitrary, omnipotent power of another."[122]

This is not how Erasmus viewed warfare. Erasmus believed all war is criminal and necessarily brings with it a "cost so great, that even if you win the war, you will lose much more than you gain."[123] It is instructive, then, to examine the root of Erasmus' thinking more closely. Johnson argues that Erasmus objected to war due to its inherent horrors, its "frivolity" and "lack of necessity," and on the grounds that it could never accomplish what some ethicists, and the JWD, say it can do, which is provide moral justification for military force. What then, are statesmen and the lesser magistrates (the American electorate) to do?

Johnson instructs that for Erasmus and his intellectual followers, a cooperative world community was an intrinsic good, achievable, and necessary aim. Grasping this argument is needed to understand the pacifist and disarmament positions. Erasmus's intellectual followers believe it is self-evident to all rational leaders that use of military force among nations cannot be condoned, and thus the aim must include global government, nuclear disarmament and the end of warfare. To use Keith Payne's description of this logic in the context of the nuclear disarmament cause: "But it is a banal tautology to say that the elimination of nuclear arms will end the threat of nuclear war. That claim is comparable to saying that universal wealth will end poverty, and universal home ownership will end homelessness."[124] The tautology may

---

[122] James W. Child, *Nuclear War: The Moral Dimension* (London: Transaction Books, Inc., 1986), p. 105.

[123] Quoted in, William V. O'Brien and John P. Langan, *The Nuclear Dilemma and the Just War Tradition* (Lexington, MA: Lexington Books, April 1986), p. 36.

[124] Keith B. Payne, "Tilting at Windmills: Nuclear Disarmament Advocacy in an Anarchic World Order," *Information Series*, No. 540 (Fairfax, VA: National Institute Press, November 22, 2022), p. 2,

be true, but it provides no useful guidance as to how to create the conditions needed to achieve the goal.

The arguments that religious scholars put forward that fit more coherently in an idealist framework are consistent with the ideological roots in the views of Erasmus. Those who appeal to the JWD but argue for idealist aims are trying to fit a square peg in a round hole; it will not fit. But in trying, they misuse the JWD and lead its well-meaning adherents down a confused and dangerous path.

Futurist and Cold War strategist Herman Kahn warned that even if this idealist world could finally become reality (a notion that belies the basic anthropological assumptions about the fallibility and too-often cruelty and brutality of man and the distrust among states that the Christian realist acknowledges) there would remain persistent problems. Kahn surmises that it would be infeasible to verify perfect compliance for nuclear disarmament.[125] If a nation did, hypothetically, decide to violate the established nuclear zero law to secure an advantage among its neighbors, a very real possibility because the invention of nuclear technology cannot be unlearned, the violating nation could have the advantage of breaking out first and coercing its neighbors with nuclear threats. The supposed global governance could not be expected to provide reliable protection, any more than any other human institute is without flaws and fully reliable. So even in this idealist aspiration, one could hardly take comfort in the expectation that peace would be everlasting. To the contrary, nations would continue to distrust others, regimes would ceaselessly pursue what they perceive as their interests, and "nuclear zero," if ever achieved, would surely be a fleeting reality.[126]

---

available at https://nipp.org/wp-content/uploads/2022/11/IS-540.pdf.

[125] Herman Kahn, *On Thermonuclear War*, (Princeton, NJ: Princeton University Press, 1960) pp. 5-7.

[126] Loc. cit.

The Atomic Age, JWD Violations,
and Nuclear Pacifism

There are modern intellectual heirs of Erasmus' world government moral imperative in the context of the atomic age. In 1983, American Catholic bishops released a long, nuanced, and influential pastoral letter on nuclear weapons.[127] The bishops concluded their letter with a rejection of vital aspects of the U.S. policy towards nuclear deterrence. Instead, the bishops, while accepting that possessing nuclear weapons was morally permissible (following Pope John Paul's lead),[128] held that nations are only morally permitted to maintain nuclear weapons for deterrence purposes as an interim measure until the day when world leaders could achieve global disarmament; the American bishops concluded that there is no morally permissible defense of their employment.

The bishops' assessment was that any employment of nuclear weapons would likely fail to meet the JWD principles of discrimination, proportionality, and probability of success. It is important to identify the assumptions on which the bishops' conclusions were predicated to evaluate similar arguments made by other prominent nuclear deterrence skeptics and disarmament advocates that remain active today.

The bishops take the subject of nuclear warfare appropriately seriously, along with their mission to inform Christian conscience and align U.S. nuclear policy with the

---

[127] National Conference on Catholic Bishops, "The Challenge of Peace: God's Promise and Our Response: A Pastoral Letter on War and Peace by the National Conference of Catholic Bishops," *U.S. Conference of Catholic Bishops* (May 3, 1983), available at https://www.usccb.org/upload/challenge-peace-gods-promise-our-response-1983.pdf. (Hereafter, *NCCB 1983 Pastoral Letter*).

[128] As referenced in Keith B. Payne, "The Bishops and Nuclear Weapons," *Orbis: A Journal of World Affairs*, Volume 27, Number 3, (Fall 1983), p. 535.

JWD. However, their first objection to U.S. nuclear strategy is against the very planning for limited use to achieve military objectives if deterrence fails. The bishops believed that it was very unlikely that nuclear war could remain limited and was likely instead to escalate to the highest levels of death, including massive civilian death. And because of this belief in the likelihood of uncontrolled escalation, the principles of discrimination and of proportionality would be violated.[129] And due to their assessment that any nuclear employment would escalate, it also would run afoul of the JWD principle of possessing a reasonable hope of success. In short, according to the bishops, initiating nuclear violence was bound to precipitate nuclear escalation that could not be controlled and almost certainly would end with holocaust.[130] According to the bishops' reasoning, if it is accepted that nuclear escalation will almost certainly occur, and that discrimination and proportionality are impossibilities, no just warrior could employ nuclear weapons and satisfy the JWD principles.

While conceding that it is impossible to know for certain what may happen in the event of a limited nuclear attack, the bishops contend that, "The burden of proof remains on those who assert that meaningful limitation is possible."[131] This is the intellectual lynchpin to their argument. They place the burden of proof on those who, like them, acknowledge that it is unknowable if limiting a nuclear war is possible, but determine that it is better to try to credibly deter and defend rather than refuse to try and thereby doom innocents to the whims of authoritarians with nuclear weapons.

---

[129] *NCCB 1983 Pastoral Letter*, op. cit., p. 29.

[130] Loc. cit., p. 29.

[131] Ibid., p. 3.

The bishops essentially opposed the employment of nuclear weapons, even in a limited manner, due to the great destructive potential of nuclear escalation. According to the bishops, it was a "perverted political policy or moral casuistry which tried to justify using a weapon which 'indirectly' or 'unintentionally' killed a million innocent people because they happened to live near a 'militarily significant target.'"[132]

To summarize, the bishops' objections to the preparation of nuclear responses if deterrence fails rely on two broad assumptions: the near certainty of nuclear escalation to highest levels of nuclear war and the inherent indiscriminateness of nuclear weapons. But there are great problems with their assumptions, and strategists and ethicists contested them at the time of the letter and continue to this day. For example, Albert Wohlstetter noted:

> The bishops cite experts as authority for their judgment that any use whatever of nuclear weapons would with an overwhelming probability lead to unlimited destruction. And some of their experts do seem to say just that. But some they cite appear only to say that we cannot be quite sure ... that any use of nuclear weapons stays limited.[133]

Wohlstetter's point is an important one. The concern about escalation is legitimate and nuclear strategists recognize it is possible. It is not a hypothetical phenomenon to be taken lightly; however, the certainty that the bishops express about nuclear escalation ignores the powerful reasons why national leaders would be highly motivated to exercise nuclear restraint and to strive to steer the adversary towards war termination on the lowest levels of violence

---

[132] Ibid., p. 35.

[133] Quoted in, O'Brien and Langan, *The Nuclear Dilemma and the Just War Tradition*, op. cit., p. 87.

possible. For example, the very fear of escalation the bishops emphasize could in fact compel the government leaders to act with restraint and dissuade them from escalating.

Payne and Coleman note: "There are a number of reasons to believe that a war began with a limited use of nuclear weapons in fact might not escalate out of control. Furthermore, there is also reason to believe that limited and discriminate nuclear use could satisfy Just War requirements. There are tremendous incentives on both sides to limit destruction in the event of a nuclear confrontation."[134]

Ramsey, agreeing with Schelling's famous contention argued in his 1962 essay "Nuclear Strategy in Europe," reminds of the unpleasant reality that in the Atomic Age, all military strikes even at low conventional levels of violence run the risk of spiraling to nuclear use. However, this presents both the possibility of nuclear employment but also a "built-in dampener" that no nation can remove.[135] This description of the built-in dampener bolsters the arguments of Payne and Coleman. Wohlstetter agrees, stressing that the apocalyptic rhetoric of the Catholic bishops is not rooted in evidence of the past or sound logical analysis. Not only does it stand to reason that a limited nuclear employment may not lead to Armageddon but as Wohlstetter also argues, a limited attack on military targets meant to minimize civilian deaths is less likely to prompt an adversary to escalate than deliberate attacks on a city meant to maximize civilian (innocent) death and suffering.[136]

O'Brien acknowledges the gravity of the concerns of those who fear that nuclear escalation is uncontrollable. He

---

[134] Keith B. Payne and Jill E. Coleman, "Christian Nuclear Pacifism and The Just War Tradition," op. cit., p. 79.

[135] Paul Ramsey, *The Just War*, op. cit., p. 254.

[136] Albert Wohlstetter, "Bishops, Statemen, and Other Strategists on the Bombing of Innocents," *Commentary* (June 1983), p. 17.

acknowledges that in theory he can imagine counterforce targeting with precisely the right weapons could neatly meet the criteria of the JWD as intended by the just government. But he also acknowledges that there are many variables that will impact the way the theory unfolds in real life and that it is entirely possible that there would be unacceptably high civilian casualties or that the enemy would respond in unpredictable and regrettable escalatory ways. He concludes, however, that there is no just alternative to preparing to attempt to convince the enemy to return to peace by preparing counterforce and damage limitation options. The alternative is to choose to remain unprepared and unwilling to protect the innocent, and thereby abdicate one's duty to protect the nation and its people, is to be culpable of facilitating the worst possible outcomes.[137]

U.S. military strategists and policymakers agreed that while there was no way to know with certainty, evidence and reason give cause to believe that a nuclear exchange would not necessarily escalate to the highest levels of violence and destruction, and that it was incumbent on the United States to have the ability and the options in a variety of contingencies to try to limit escalation. And, if the bishops and those who agreed with them had their way, and the United States refused to maintain the possibility of engaging in limited, counterforce response options with an eye toward steering the enemy to stand down and end the war, the plausible alternative is to maintain a countervalue force with the highly destructive and indiscriminate results the bishops fear escalation would reach. As strategist Colin Gray noted, the strategist who embraces a counterforce flexible posture does not exclude the possibility of catastrophe, but understands that mutual vulnerability maintained by counter-city targeting without defenses

---

[137] See William V. O'Brien, "Just War Doctrine in a Nuclear Context," op. cit., p. 200.

guarantees the most horrible catastrophes if deterrence fails.[138]

By the time the United States was locked in the Cold War with the Soviet Union and no longer possessed the strategic nuclear superiority it enjoyed in the early decades after the Second World War, U.S. civilian leaders recognized a need to reevaluate U.S. nuclear deterrence policy and strategy.

In 1974, James Schlesinger, President Richard Nixon's Secretary of Defense, called for refining the target list and selective targeting against enemies in the event of war. This led to the dramatic formalization and "evolutionary refinement" of U.S. nuclear deterrence policy that would provide options to employ nuclear weapons in a more credible, limited way if deterrence failed.[139] This evolutionary refinement and codification of U.S. policy will be discussed more fully in Chapter 4. But the point should be understood that the Catholic bishops were expressing concern about escalation that had been considered seriously by U.S. government and military strategists. But the bishops had negligible confidence in the agency of the men who would make military decisions about how to respond to attack and prosecute a war in defense of the American people and their vital interests. For the bishops, limited nuclear employment seemed highly unlikely considering that such factors as the duress and confusion of the moment could overtake the men and inevitably lead to world destruction.[140]

The bishops' second assumption, that the intentional avoidance of civilian targeting and the targeting of strictly military targets could not satisfy the JWD principle of

---

[138] See Colin S. Gray, *Nuclear Strategy and Strategic Planning,* op. cit., p. 62.

[139] O'Brien and Langan, *The Nuclear Dilemma and the Just War Tradition,* op. cit., p. 88.

[140] *NCCB 1983 Pastoral Letter,* op. cit., p. 29.

discrimination, should also be evaluated. When scientific studies and modeling have been conducted — considering the technical characteristics of various delivery systems and variable yields, as well as the way weapons are employed and where the military targets are located — the potential civilian casualties vary greatly. Not only do they vary, but the difference between deliberately attacking a civilian target — a clear and egregious violation of the JWD of discrimination — and seeking to attack a military target while also seeking to limit the damage of civilians also can be vast. For example, a 2001 Natural Resources Defense Council study showed that the difference in casualties between striking a military target set versus a societal target set was in the tens of millions.[141] To be sure, a strike that results in millions of deaths is a horror, but much less so than one that results in the death of ten times as many civilian lives. There have been many more studies since the Cold War that show that if the nuclear attacker is trying to minimize casualties, it certainly can be done.[142]

The bishops and contemporary commentators who stress the potential maximum effect of nuclear weapon and who would agree with the desirability of preserving innocents are eliding the physical and mathematical facts. The degree of innocent loss of life and suffering is greatly

---

[141] Matthew G. McKinzie, Thomas B. Cochran, Robert S. Norris, and William M. Arkin, *The U.S. Nuclear War Plan: A Time for Change* (Washington, DC: Natural Resources Defense Council, June 2001), p. 130, available at https://www.nrdc.org/sites/default/files/us-nuclear-war-plan-report.pdf.

[142] See data in testimony of Secretary of Defense James Schlesinger in U.S. Senate, Committee on Foreign Relations, Subcommittee on Arms Control, International Law and Organization, *Briefing on Counterforce Attacks*, 93rd Congress, 2nd Session, September 11, 1974, p. 26. Schlesinger provides supporting analysis for his conclusion presented on p. 26, "In a carefully planned attack, however, one can reduce those collateral mortalities significantly, if that is one of the attacker's objectives."

affected by the method of targeting, and the principles of discrimination and proportionality are not obviated because of the known possibility of civilian death, even significant civilian death. The bishops set a standard in the context of nuclear deterrence that even non-nuclear war could not meet in the real world. Indeed, the reality of nuclear weapons raises the stakes for ensuring U.S. nuclear deterrence and is credible. And yet the bishops are unwilling to approve of what is required to achieve and maintain it.

The American Catholic bishops recognized that unilateral disarmament carried a risk too great and so they could not embrace it. But, revealing a tortured logic, they also concluded that the necessary path forward was a form of world government that would enforce global disarmament.[143] Specifically, they advocated "some form of global authority adequate to the needs of the international common good."[144] One does wonder how the bishops were so sure that the men charged with making decisions in war are so deeply flawed that they would precipitate Armageddon in a fit of error, rage and fear, and yet simultaneously so consistent, rational and benevolent as to believe in the real possibility they could achieve global disarmament and establish a reliably benevolent form of world government.

To summarize, the bishops opposed nuclear targeting of both societal objects and military/state control objects and state their view that they could not perceive any contingency that would provide a morally licit reason to initiate nuclear employment, and strongly suggest (but do not explicitly say) that they oppose any use of nuclear weapons, even in limited scenarios. Without offering any possibility wherein employment is morally justified, the

---

[143] John W. Coffey in "Deterrence and the Bishops: A Trans-Atlantic Comparison," *Strategic Review*, Vol. 14, No. 1 (Winter 1986), p. 64.

[144] *NCCB 1983 Pastoral Letter*, op. cit., p. 3.

bishops appear to support nuclear possession for deterrence purposes but never for employment.[145] They are, in other words, nuclear pacifists. If we are to adhere to Child's logic, that nuclear pacifism is effectively submission to slavery, then we are on solid ground for noting that the bishops' conclusions, if policymakers adhered to them, could lead to acquiescence to the diktats of the Russian or North Korean regimes or to the Chinese Communist Party rather than deterring them from military conquest.

The German and the French Roman Catholic episcopacies issued their own pastoral letters on nuclear deterrence after the American bishops released theirs. John W. Coffey explains that the view of many experts was that the German and the French letters offered more prudent responses than the American bishops because at least the former could see clearly enough the evil of authoritarian regimes confronting the West. The American bishops, rather than faulting the evil of authoritarian regimes, faulted the nuclear weapons themselves, regardless of the nature of the regime that possesses them.[146] (This was one of O'Brien's criticisms of the American bishops' pastoral letter. He observed that they left out discussion about the nature of the totalitarian threat to the United States and the free world, a discussion O'Brien argues is vital before one can assess various JWD criteria.[147])

The twin emphases of arms control and disarmament enforced by world government is consistent with the idealist and not the realist framework. But the realist — and the just warrior — appreciates Coffey's warning against the danger of basing policies on the hope of a "chimerical" world government given the persistent absence of two necessary conditions. The first necessary condition as

---

[145] Ibid., pp. 27-28.

[146] Coffey, "Deterrence and the Bishops," op. cit., pp. 60-61.

[147] O'Brien, "Just War Doctrine in a Nuclear Context," op. cit., p. 200.

elucidated by Coffey is a "global political and moral community binding all men together and underlying that government manifestly does not exist."[148] Coffey goes on to outline all the ways governments and national identities are formed. They are formed throughout history through experiences, events, the idiosyncratic formation of habits, and particular characters. The second necessary condition that is lacking is a global consensus regarding what constitutes justice or the common good. During the Cold War, the Scowcroft Commission delivered to the president on April 6, 1983, the *Report on the President's Commission on Strategic Forces* that illustrated the absence of such a consensus. The report articulated the conflicting natures of the Soviet Union and the United States and the Western world and helpfully clarified the nature of what was at stake and the importance of formulating a policy and strategy for strategic deterrence. It said:

> Although the United States and the Soviet Union hold fundamentally incompatible views of history, of the nature of society, and of the individual's place in it, the existence of nuclear weapons imbues that rivalry with peril unprecedented in human history. The temptation is sometimes great to simplify — or oversimplify — the difficult problems that result, either by blinking at the devasting nature of modern full-scale war or by refusing to acknowledge the emptiness of life under modern totalitarianism. ... [O]ur task as a nation cannot be understood from a position of moral neutrality toward the differences between liberty and totalitarianism. These differences proceed from conflicting views regarding the rights of individuals and the nature of society. Only if Americans believe that it is

---

148 Coffey, p. 65.

worth a sustained effort over the years to preserve liberal values can our task be seen as a just and worthy one in spite of its dangers.[149]

As discussed above, war breaks out among nations because of persistent distrust among them, and, as articulated by Coffey, their conflicting goals and views of the good.[150] Coffey admonishes, "Even a united world, then, would not be a disarmed one — that is, unless one imagines a species of humans starkly different from the present one."[151] Arms control or disarmament enforced by world government elides the root problems and therefore cannot offer a more harmonious outcome or solve the problems that lead to conflict and war.

Recall that this study previously established that the JWD guides the just nation and warrior within a realist framework. It is important to observe at this point, then, that although the American bishops (and their European brethren) employ the JWD principles throughout their nuanced pastoral letters, their analyses reflect an idealist perspective and aims. The contradictions within the bishops' letters arise from their seeking to apply tools for just war designed for a realists' view of the international system and not for the idealists' view of the international system.

But what about the possibility of maintaining a force along the lines of what the bishops seemed to be most comfortable with? One that rejects the possibility of even preparing for limited nuclear employment, for deterrence purposes only, would be a force designed to keep the possibility of a nuclear exchange as terrifying as possible

---

[149] President's Commission on Strategic Forces, Report of the President's Commission On Strategic Forces (Washington, D.C.), April 1983, pp. 2-3, available at https://web.mit.edu/chemistry/deutch/policy/1983-ReportPresCommStrategic.pdf.

[150] Coffey, "Deterrence and the Bishops," op. cit., p. 65.

[151] Ibid., p. 66.

rather than leaving the military strategists with the option to act with restraint in the event an adversary attacked vital U.S. interests. O'Brien convincingly rules out the "MAD [Mutually Assured Destruction] threat" as one that would intentionally violate the principle of discrimination if implemented. He points out that some, but only few, have argued that MAD is permissible if there is a "secret resolve" to not carry through with the threat if deterrence breaks down. In other words, some argue that MAD might be permissible morally if it is a grand bluff. But, O'Brien says, returning to his axiom, deterrence relies on the adversary's belief that there is truly a will to make good on the threat.[152]

But could the defender sufficiently convince the adversary that his deterrent threat is credible? The defender could maintain a nuclear force and either imply or perhaps even explicitly threaten to use it under extreme circumstances, even though he was convinced that there would never be a morally licit or defense to carry through with the explicit or implied threats. Ramsey, a one-time exponent of the bluff strategy, went on to disavow it.[153] Indeed, in *The Case for Making Just War Possible*, Ramsey explains that plans to not follow through on the promises of retaliation would eventually come to light, possibly due to a leaker. But, even if no person leaked the truth of the bluff, Ramsey says that our "philosophic objection" would become evident in U.S. behaviors because we would lack the "courage of rashness."[154] Herman Kahn famously

---

[152] William V. O'Brien, *The Conduct of Just and Limited War*, op. cit., pp. 138-139.

[153] Ibid., p. 138.

[154] Paul Ramsey, "The Case for Making 'Just War' Possible," in, John Bennett, ed., *Nuclear Weapons and the Conflict of Conscience* (New York, NY: Charles Scribner and Sons, 1962), p. 167.

quipped, "Usually the most convincing way to look willing is to be willing."[155]

The success of deterrence relies on the adversary's belief that the act of aggression he is considering is likely to elicit a punitive response so great that it would cause him to regret the initial act of aggression or a response that would deny him the goals of the aggression. So, the prudent defender cannot afford to orchestrate a bluff. There are too many possibilities for the bluff to be exposed, and should that happen in matters of nuclear war, the costs would be catastrophic. Perhaps even more fundamentally, it is incredible to suggest that an open society such as the United States could train thousands of personnel and perennially devote the resources needed to maintain, and exercise weapons required to sustain an elaborate bluff, with only a few knowing that this costly effort is a secret bluff. The problem is not just that the reality of a bluff would leak, it is that how you prepare in many nuanced and sophisticated ways, and how you train thousands for war, will determine the options available when you fight. Referencing Kahn's 1960 book *On Thermonuclear War*, Ramsey points to the wisdom of preparing to engage militarily—whatever that might mean—if deterrence fails. Preparing to fight and win, so goes Ramsey's and Kahn's argument, bolsters the credibility of deterrence in the mind of the adversary.[156] The robust preparation needed to credibly prepare for war while actually holding to a bluff strategy simply cannot coexist over the long term, especially as different governments come and go.

Payne and Coleman also counter that it is not probable that Congress would fund a "Potemkin" nuclear force.[157]

---

[155] Quoted in Payne and Coleman, "Christian Nuclear Pacifism and The Just War Tradition," op. cit., p. 78.

[156] Ramsey, *The Just War*, op. cit., pp. 174-175.

[157] Payne and Coleman, "Christian Nuclear Pacifism and The Just War Tradition," op. cit., p. 78.

O'Brien warns that, "A Western deterrent that is practically and morally unusable as a war-fighting instrument if deterrence fails is not stable."[158]

Payne points out that the American Catholic bishops' willingness to allow nuclear weapons but never their employment is exactly the kind of bluff that he, O'Brien and Ramsey demonstrate is incoherent, unworkable, and far too risky.[159] O'Brien surmises, "Perhaps influenced by nuclear nominalism, the bishops want to have deterrence without those elements of intention and will that are indispensable to deterrence."[160]

Paul Ramsey explains that the JWD has fashioned rules for *practical conduct* (emphasis mine) that at once justify war and limit it.[161] Harkening to O'Brien's point, planning for deterrence is not an abstract exercise and "nuclear nominalism" is unserious and very risky. Ramsey goes on, "We want our nation's policies to be moral as well as prudent. Indeed, our purpose is to construct a moral theory that justifies a nuclear defense policy, and that is *ipso facto* a moral enterprise."[162]

The bishops opposed targeting societies, on grounds that that would indisputably violate the principle of discrimination. This view was shared by others like O'Brien, who support nuclear deterrence on moral grounds, and agree with the American bishops that it is morally impermissible to intentionally launch a nuclear attack against a population center filled with civilians. He says that while better and clearer discrimination is possible, when there are numerous military targets available, it is not

---

[158] O'Brien and Langan, *The Nuclear Dilemma and the Just War Tradition*, op. cit., p. 175.

[159] Payne, "The Bishops and Nuclear Weapons," op. cit., p. 539.

[160] William V. O'Brien, "A Just War Deterrence/Defense Strategy," *Center Journal* (Winter 1983), p. 11.

[161] Ramsey, "The Case for Making 'Just War' Possible," op. cit., p. 146.

[162] Child, *Nuclear War: The Moral Dimension*, op. cit., p. 78.

credible to argue that an intentional countervalue attack on a city would meet the JWD discrimination demands that the attack minimize the evil involved.[163]

The bishops assert that planning for the possibility of nuclear employment would "encourage notions that nuclear war can be engaged in with tolerable human and moral consequences."[164] Thus, the bishops conclude that nuclear deterrence can only be comprised of a capability that is "sufficient to deter" and cannot be superior to adversaries' nuclear weapons forces. The reasoning of the bishops results in a logical collision. The bishops forbid any employment of nuclear use but permit the possession of nuclear weapons only "sufficient to deter" an enemy. This forces the conclusion that the bishops recommend having a sufficient nuclear weapons capability to deter, but also warn that employment is never morally permissible; this inescapably leaves a nuclear buff that is unlikely to deter reliably.

Mainline Protestant Churches Oppose Nuclear Deterrence

While the focus in this chapter has rested on the American Catholic bishops' pastoral letter, the bishops were certainly not the only Christian leaders during the Cold War to reject nuclear employment under any circumstances. The United Methodist, Presbyterian, United Church of Christ, Reformed Church of America, and American Lutheran denominations did as well.[165] None of the churches' statements, including the bishops' letter, are binding on religious adherents but should be understood as moral

---

[163] O'Brien, *The Conduct of Just and Limited War*, op. cit., p. 137.

[164] *NCCB 1983 Pastoral Letter*, op. cit., p. 24.

[165] Payne and Coleman, "Christian Nuclear Pacifism and The Just War Tradition," op. cit., p. 75.

guidance.[166] Of the various main Protestant churches in the United States that have issued statements on nuclear weapons, most use language reflective of the JWD principles, and offer advice that similarly emphasizes deterrence, arms control, and aspirations for disarmament.

Of note, the Lutheran Church-Missouri Synod and the Southern Baptist Convention (SBC) at the time of the Cold War and to this day reflect what could be characterized as the most emphatic view of a strong defense and rejection of pacifism towards the Christian aim of peacemaking.[167] However, the current head of the Catholic Church, Pope Francis, has gone beyond the earlier nuanced bishops' 1983 pastoral letter. Pope Francis has declared the employment and the possession of nuclear weapons "immoral."[168] The Vatican Foreign Minister Dominique Mamberti has called policies of nuclear deterrence an "obstacle" to nuclear disarmament.[169] Keith Payne responds to the modern

---

[166] Donald Davidson, *Nuclear Weapons and the American Churches: Ethical Positions on Modern Warfare* (Boulder, CO: Westview Press, 1983), p. 117.

[167] Ibid., p. 162.

[168] Macy Sullivan, "Pope Francis: Nuclear Weapons are Immoral," Catholic News Agency, June 21, 2022, available at https://www.catholicnewsagency.com/news/251596/pope-francis-nuclear-weapons-are-immoral. For a summary of Pope Francis' views on nuclear weapons and the challenge of squaring them with the Just War Doctrine, see Heather Williams, "Ultima Ratio: Papal Statements on Nuclear Weapons and the Just War Doctrine," in *Morality and Nuclear Weapons: Practitioner Perspectives*, ed. Brad Roberts (Livermore: Center for Global Security Research, 2023), pp. 42-58, available at https://cgsr.llnl.gov/content/assets/docs/CGSR-Occasional_Paper_MoralityandNuclearWeapons_06302023.pdf.

[169] Statement of the Holy See, as delivered by H.E. Dominique Mamberti, Secretary for the Holy See's Relations with States, at the High-level Meeting of the 68th Session of the General Assembly on Nuclear Disarmament in New York (September 26, 2013), available at https://www.vatican.va/content/dam/wss/roman_curia/secretariat_state/2013/documents/rc-seg-st-20130926_mamberti-nuclear-disarmament_en.html.

categorical church-based objections to nuclear employment, possession, and indeed deterrence:

> Because a credible policy of nuclear deterrence depends on the possession of nuclear weapons and a sufficiently believable threat to employ them under some circumstances, it is unsurprising that the church-based reports and positions that generally reject the employment and the possession of nuclear weapons as immoral also reject nuclear deterrence as immoral and identify nuclear disarmament as the alternative.[170]

As radical as the bishops' and other church leaders' conclusions were in the 1980s, they did permit the maintenance of U.S. nuclear weapons at least for a notion of deterrence purposes, as a temporary solution to the nuclear dangers. Others went even further, as the current Catholic Church leaders do now, and employed just war arguments to advocate for disarmament and against any maintenance of nuclear weapons, even temporarily.

Ronald J. Sider and Richard K. Taylor's influential 1982 book, *Nuclear Holocaust and Christian Hope: A Book for Christian Peacemakers*, explains this position well. Sider and Taylor advanced the arguments that nuclear war was highly unlikely, if not impossible, to control. They worried about possible accidents that could lead to nuclear employment, problems with communications between the government authorities and the military operators, and they worried that any nuclear employment would necessarily elicit a nuclear response, and during the "pressure" of the war both sides would continue to escalate to the highest

---

[170] Keith B. Payne, *Chasing a Grand Illusion,* op. cit., p. 13.

levels of thermonuclear employment.[171] For Sider and Taylor, no just government could ever employ a nuclear weapon due to their belief of inevitable nuclear escalation, and therefore no just government could morally build and maintain a nuclear deterrence force because it might tempt the first employment of a nuclear weapon that would necessarily lead to unlimited nuclear escalation.

But Sider and Taylor, like many of the influential opponents of U.S. nuclear deterrence, have misplaced confidence in their assumption of the inevitability of uncontrolled escalation. We can never know with certainty what the response of an adversary will be — and the United States always retains its agency in how it will respond. Choosing to take off the table the possibility of a U.S. nuclear response would likely give the adversary confidence that it could more easily secure its military and political aims if it employs a nuclear weapon. Therefore, embracing Sider's and Taylor's refusal to consider a nuclear response under any circumstances creates an unacceptably high risk of deterrence failure, and even nuclear war.

Sider and Taylor then go to reexamine the presuppositions of the JWD. They turn to the New Testament and specifically the words of Christ before the Roman Governor of Judaea, Pontius Pilate, the earthly authority who would adjudicate Christ's alleged crimes. In John 18:36 Christ tells Pilate, "My kingship is not of this world; if my kingship were of this world, my servants would fight, that I might not be handed over to the Jews; but my Kingship is not of this world." Sider and Taylor explain that they believe that Jesus was bringing about a new authority to the fallen world that superseded the fallen order. This new authority did not permit violence of any kind. They concluded that the life of any Christian must be

---

[171] Ronald J. Sider and Richard K Taylor, *Nuclear Holocaust and Christian Hope: A Book for Christian Peacemakers*, (Downers Grove, IL: Intervarsity Press, 1982), p. 73.

one of nonviolence. Putting an honest and fine point on their striking conclusion, they write, "Fighting—even defensive violence to prevent the most unjust arrest in human history—belongs to the sinful order. Jesus's followers, however, must live according to the new norms of the messianic age. Therefore, Jesus says, they will not fight."[172]

For Sider and Taylor, there is no duality between the government authorities and the private citizen. They believe that Christian teaching rejects the distinction between government and private citizens explicitly and outright.[173] Therefore, according to Sider and Taylor, the only conclusion for the followers of Christian teaching is to take up the way of nonviolence and to become a pacifist and nuclear abolitionist. They insist that just as Christians worked to speed the abolition of the slavery, the modern cause should be the cause of global nuclear disarmament.[174] The authors conclude their book with an emotional plea not to massively kill our enemies in the nuclear age, but to massively love them.[175] However, sincere desire does not necessarily result in just outcomes. The pacifism Sider and Taylor passionately extol in the nuclear age would create a context in which aggressive nuclear powers with the intent to supplant the United States and the US-led order could dominate all others with the likelihood of catastrophic nuclear violence, destruction, and human death and suffering as a result. Preventing this result is precisely what the nuclear pacifists say is what they wish to avoid and refuse to participate in, and yet the policy they advocate would increase its likelihood.

---

[172] Ibid., p. 108.

[173] Ibid., p. 114.

[174] Ibid., p. 193.

[175] Ibid., p. 292.

Chapter Four: Making Nuclear Deterrence Strategy More Credible

"The defense policy of the United States is based on a simple premise: The United States does not start fights. We will never be an aggressor. We maintain our strength in order to deter and defend against aggression – to preserve freedom and peace."
— *President Reagan, March, 1983*

For more than seven decades, the United States has sought to sustain credible nuclear deterrence, including adjusting to accommodate changes in the threat environment.[176] Over the years and across administrations the United States continued to alter its nuclear weapons force by decreasing the numbers of certain deployed systems, eliminating entire categories of weapons, and choosing to cease explosive nuclear testing. It has also added systems, modernized aging systems, increased the penetration ability and accuracy of weapons, and sought to improve the quality of the nuclear weapons enterprise. Within the broader umbrella of strategic deterrence, U.S. conventional forces have also gone through evolutions, as have nuclear policies and strategies. However, regardless of the changes, the definition of deterrence and its requirements were refined throughout the Cold War and to this day.

The bipartisan 1983 Scowcroft Commission offers a timeless description of the nature of deterrence and how the strategist must endeavor to deter U.S. adversaries:

---

[176] For a brief explanation of the continuity of the aim of U.S. nuclear deterrence, see Franklin Miller, "American Nuclear Deterrence Policy: What Is It and How Is It Implemented?" in *A Guide To Nuclear Deterrence in the Age of Great Power Competition*, ed. Adam Lowther (Bossier City: Louisiana Tech Research Institute, 2020), at Guide-to-Nuclear-Deterrence-in-the-Age-of-Great-Power-Competition-Lowther.pdf (atloa.org).

> In order for deterrence to be effective we must not merely have weapons, we must be perceived to be able, and prepared, if necessary, to use them effectively against the key elements of [an enemy's] power. Deterrence is not an abstract notion amenable to simple quantification. Still less is it a mirror of what would deter ourselves. Deterrence is the set of beliefs in the minds of the [enemy] leaders, given their own values and attitudes, about our capabilities and our will. It requires us to determine, as best we can, what would deter them from considering aggression, even in a crisis — not to determine what would deter us.[177]

The targets within the key elements of an enemy's power will be specific for the deterrence of different foes, as will assessments about the enemy's perception of what Washington is willing and able to do to thwart its aims or harm its interests if deterrence fails and the enemy decides to attack U.S. core interests. This is referred to as "tailoring" deterrence to the specific character of the enemy and context.

As the threats have changed, whether those changes have manifested in the U.S. assessment of the relationship between the U.S. and other nations, or in the capabilities of nations that were previously not hostile and became hostile, the United States has also sought to adapt its force posture and nuclear weapons complex to ensure it meets the requirements necessary to deter each adversary.

The requirements for maintaining the deterrence policy are fulfilled in a variety of ways, including by building and maintaining the appropriate strategic deterrence force; maintaining and adapting the associated nuclear weapons

---

[177] President's Commission on Strategic Forces, Report of the President's Commission On Strategic Forces, op. cit., pp. 2-3.

enterprise, and issuing public statements and clarifying official policies such as the declaratory policy regarding deterrence threats and "redlines." The principles of deterrence are unchanging, but the United States must adapt the application of those principles because U.S. adversaries and their national aims, interests, and alliances; their weapons, and their elements of societal control are dynamic.

Because adversaries are dynamic, so are the potential targets that the United States may need to credibly hold at risk with nuclear weapons. The number of targets may grow and the adversaries' dedication to defending those targets may create obstacles for the United States to credibly hold those targets at risk. Geopolitical changes as well as U.S. adversaries' military improvements have driven U.S. changes in its nuclear deterrence force structure—so that military leaders can credibly persuade adversaries that the United States has the capability to thwart whatever perceived gain the adversary believes it will achieve by attacking U.S. interests.[178]

At the same time, the United States has sought to adapt its nuclear posture, add or subtract the numbers or categories of nuclear weapons, add active or passive defenses, and improve the technical ability of U.S. strategic delivery systems. The United States has also, as a matter of U.S. policy, endeavored to maintain *moral* deterrence options even as it improves and modernizes military deterrence options. This is evident in more than just public press releases or presidential statements. Hewing closely to consistent and historic U.S. views of what is morally licit in warfare and adapting offensive and defensive weapons to

---

[172] For a concise history of the sequence of presidential directives and memoranda that articulated this strategy to deny the adversary victory, see, National Institute for Public Policy, "Special Issue: Deterring China in the Taiwan Strait," *Journal of Policy & Strategy*, Vol. 2, No. 2, National Institute Press, 2022, p. 37.

sustain the credibility of deterrence have occurred in tandem.

As William O'Brien instructed, "[B]y far the most important sources of proper conduct in war are the plans, strategies, orders, missions, force compositions, and weapon systems development decisions that determine the nature of wars."[179] Heeding O'Brien's direction, to analyze the U.S. view of proper conduct in war as it pertains to U.S. nuclear weapons, this study turns to official government policy and planning documents, including Congressional testimony and associated studies as well as official government memoranda and directives.

Although military planners during the Harry S. Truman years initiated U.S. nuclear targeting and planning, through 1948 the only official, publicly-expressed national policies on nuclear weapons were that they would be civilian controlled.[180] Truman left office still firmly believing that nuclear weapons were political weapons of last resort but without having established official national policy on nuclear strategy and deterrence.[181] President Dwight D. Eisenhower developed plans that were described as being intended to maximize destruction and to generate the highest degree of capability.[182] The Kennedy Administration publicly expressed a desire to have more options than Eisenhower's nuclear strategy of "Massive Retaliation."[183] This was the first rhetorical U.S. break from targeting cities to flexible counterforce targeting and

---

[179] William V. O'Brien, *The Conduct of Just and Limited War*, op. cit., p. 357.

[180] David Alan Rosenberg, "US Nuclear War Planning (1945-1960)," in *Strategic Nuclear Targeting*, ed. Desmond Ball and Jeffrey Richelson (Ithica, NY: Cornell University Press, 1986) p. 38.

[181] Ibid., p. 43.

[182] Ibid., p. 56.

[183] Desmond Ball, "The Development of the SIOP, 1960-1983," in *Strategic Nuclear Targeting*, op. cit., p. 62.

keeping the destruction of cities and populations to a minimum. However, Secretary of Defense Robert McNamara assessed that to sufficiently deter the Soviets, the United States required enough nuclear weapons to destroy 25-30% of the Soviet population and 50-75% of the Soviet industrial capacity.[184] This paradigm of "Assured Destruction" and what became known as "Mutual Assured Destruction" was the declared U.S. nuclear deterrence posture throughout the 1960s and early 1970s.

Even so, while this was the official public stance, U.S. targeting plans always included a mix of military, adversary leadership, and industrial economic targets throughout the Soviet Union. Those targets were chosen in part because the Soviet urban-industrial centers were most easily locatable, and the first U.S. nuclear delivery systems were Air Force bombers.[185]

The Soviet nuclear threat forced a breakthrough in the U.S. approach towards credibly tailoring nuclear deterrence. Moscow undertook a major expansion in the size of its nuclear warheads arsenal, introduced an operational nuclear ballistic missile submarine, and expanded its theater-range nuclear weapons.[186] As the Soviet nuclear capability expanded, it became clearer to

---

[184] See David J. Trachtenberg, "Mischaracterizing U.S. Nuclear Deterrence Policy: The Myth of Deliberate Civilian Targeting," *Information Series*, No. 542 (Fairfax, VA: National Institute Press, December 14, 2022), available at https://nipp.org/information_series/david-j-trachtenberg-mischaracterizing-u-s-nuclear-deterrence-policy-the-myth-of-deliberate-civilian-targeting-no-542-december-14-2022/.

[185] Franklin C. Miller, "Establishing the Ground Rules for Civilian Oversight," in *Managing U.S. Nuclear Operations in the 21st Century*, ed. Charles Glaser, et al., (Washington, DC: Brookings Institution Press, 2022), pp. 53-54.

[186] Miller, "Establishing the Ground Rules for Civilian Oversight," op. cit., p. 57.

civilian leaders and military planners that the U.S. needed to refine its nuclear deterrence strategy.

With Secretary of Defense James Schlesinger at the helm of the Pentagon, President Richard Nixon asked for a comprehensive review of nuclear targeting policy in National Security Study Memorandum 169 (NSSM 169), which led to the creation of a panel of experts led by Dr. John Foster. The Foster Commission's report, officially titled the Inter-Agency Working Group on NSSM 169, was the basis for National Security Decision Memorandum 242 (NSDM 242). The Foster Commission Report concluded that targeting for the purposes of deterrence requirements should hold at risk targets critical for the Soviet Union's postwar power and recovery, which would deny Moscow its theory of victory. This target list went beyond those urban, industrial, and economic resources critical to the enemy's national and military recovery and added the enemy's strategic weapon systems and included the enemy regime and its control apparatus.[187]

Nixon issued NSDM 242 on January 17, 1974. NSDM 242 clarified and made explicit that U.S. policy included counter-regime and counter-weapons targeting and flexible response options. In pursuit of options beyond massive retaliation, Nixon wanted varied nuclear weapons options for potential differing scenarios as well as the ability to limit the damage to the United States in the event of war by controlling escalation. i.e., intra-war deterrence. It stated:

> Should conflict occur, the most critical employment objective is to seek early war termination, on terms acceptable to the United States and its allies, at the lowest level of conflict feasible. This objective requires planning a wide

---

[187] Summary Report of the Inter-Agency Working Group on NSSM 169 (Washington, D.C.: The White House, June 1973), (*the Foster Panel Report*), p. 14.

range of limited nuclear employment options which could be used in conjunction with supporting political and military measures (including conventional forces) to control escalation.

Plans should be developed for limited employment options which enable the United States to conduct selected nuclear operations, in concert with conventional forces, which protect vital U. S. interests and limited enemy's ability to continue aggression. In addition, these options should enable the United States to communicate to the enemy a determination to resist aggression, coupled with a desire to exercise restraint.

Thus, options should be developed in which the level, scope, and duration of violence is limited in a manner which can be clearly and credibly communicated to the enemy. The options should (a) hold some vital enemy targets hostage to subsequent destruction by survivable nuclear forces, and (b) permit control over the timing and pace of attack execution, in order to provide the enemy opportunities to reconsider his actions.[188]

Secretary of Defense James Schlesinger articulated the clarification of U.S. policy in his testimony before Congress on March 4, 1974. In his testimony, Schlesinger sought to lay to rest misconceptions held by public officials, public commentators, and the public about the aim, and the effect, of U.S. nuclear deterrence policy and force posture. The misconceptions rested on an assumption that by increasing the number of nuclear weapons and by seeking to hold at

---

[188] President Richard Nixon, "National Security Decision Memorandum 242" (January 17, 1974), available at
https://www.nixonlibrary.gov/sites/default/files/virtuallibrary/docu
ments/nsdm/nsdm_242.pdf.

risk the adversary's warfighting apparatus, the U.S. was preparing for nuclear warfighting and thereby making nuclear warfighting more and not less likely.[189]

In testimony before the Senate Subcommittee on Arms Control, International Law and Organization of the Committee on Foreign Relations, on September 11, 1974, Schlesinger responded to questioning by Senator Edmund Muskie (D-ME), about the purpose of tactical nuclear weapons[190] as a category of weapons in the suite of weapons that constituted the flexible, accurate force Schlesinger was defending. Muskie wanted to know more about the circumstances under which the United States would employ the nuclear weapons. As often is the case, Muskie's questioning moved quickly from the primary mission of U.S. nuclear weapons—to deter—to the circumstances under which the United States might employ those weapons. Those questions are legitimate, but they often seem to be missing the larger and more critical point that the primary purpose of nuclear weapons is to deter an initial act of aggression. As Schlesinger stressed, the critical questions should focus on how nuclear weapons serve that purpose in the minds of U.S. adversaries.

Indeed, Schlesinger urged Muskie and the committee to look at the weapons from the perspective of the U.S. adversary. He said, "Looking at it from the Soviet perspective, any possibility of their employment, whether it is 3, 4, 5, percent, has a deterrent effect. We do not have to have a 100 percent confidence on our part that we would

---

[189] See U.S. Congress, Senate, Committee on Foreign Relations, Briefing by Secretary of Defense James R. Schlesinger on Casualties and Destruction Expected to Result from So-Called Nuclear Counterforce Attacks Against Military Installations in the United States: Hearing before the Committee on Foreign Relations, 93rd Congress, 2nd Session, September 11, 1974.

[190] The word tactical in this context signifies weapons that can be delivered in the regional theater, with greater accuracy and more precision.

actually employ them. As long as our opponents perceive there is some likelihood, even a low likelihood of employment, that will have a restraining influence."[191] But if the United States possessed only a relatively smaller number of nuclear weapons meant to target cities, the United States would surely be loath to employ them in response to anything but an existential attack. Consequently, the credibility of the U.S. deterrent would be limited for any other type of threat.

Consider, for example, if, in a non-nuclear conflict, an adversary threatened to employ a nuclear weapon against U.S. forces abroad or against a U.S. ally. The United States would want a deterrence threat that is credible in the minds of the adversary, and one that would demonstrate both resolve and restraint, to end the conflict on the lowest levels of violence rather than immediately escalating to the highest levels of destruction and violence. To provide a credible response, the United States would want options that seek to convince the adversary to cease the violence, while reserving more options if the adversary does not choose to de-escalate or otherwise end the war. If the U.S. only possessed or threatened massive nuclear retaliation in response to an adversary's limited nuclear employment, adversaries would likely understand that threat to be incredible in many circumstances, which could tempt adversary aggression and a failure of deterrence.

Still, Senators expressed skepticism that any U.S. nuclear employment would have meaningful variations of death and destruction, especially civilian death and destruction. Schlesinger was unflinching in his acknowledgment of the devastation of any kind of nuclear employment but also was insistent that many variables would affect the level of potential civilian death and

---

[191] U.S. Congress, Senate, Foreign Relations, Counterforce Attacks, op. cit., p. 35.

destructiveness, including the location of the intended target and the way the weapon of choice is delivered.

Schlesinger explained that a Soviet attack on U.S. ICBM silos (1,000 of them at the time) with 1,000 one megaton warheads could cause about 2.4 million casualties (800,000 fatalities). He contrasted this with a hypothetical Soviet attack on New York City, which at the time had a population of 7 million. In both instances, the civilian deaths are tragic, but an intentional attack on cities would cause far more loss of innocent life than a counterforce-oriented strike.[192]

A 1979 report by the Office of Technology Assessment,[193] not known for a rosy outlook on any kind of nuclear exchange, bolstered Schlesinger's arguments. Its analysis concluded that yes, it was possible to minimize and maximize civilian death by choosing to target military sites or cities respectively, and that targeting military sites would likely cause millions fewer deaths. Another more recent study, a 2001 assessment by the Natural Resources Defense Council, supported the previous findings and made an even starker point: Through the choice of targets, and the employment of weapons, a few hundred strategic nuclear weapons against societal targets could take the lives of 30-45 million human beings.[194] The same study found a counterforce/counter military attack with 1,300 nuclear weapons could result in far fewer estimated fatalities (11-17

---

[192] Ibid., p. 35.

[193] U.S. Congress, Office of Technology Assessment, *The Effects of Nuclear War* (Washington, D.C.: Government Printing Office, 1979), available at https://digital.library.unt.edu/ark:/67531/metadc39401/m2/1/high_res_d/7906.pdf.

[194] Matthew G. McKinzie, Thomas B. Cochran, Robert S. Norris, and William M. Arkin, *The U.S. Nuclear War Plan: A Time for Change*, op. cit., p. 130.

million casualties, the majority fatalities) than the attack against societal targets. [195]

To reiterate a critical point made throughout this study but in a slightly different way: deterrence hinges on the adversary's assessment of U.S. willingness and ability to strike what the adversary values most. Not only must the adversary make a calculation about the U.S. will to attack the adversary, he must assess that the U.S. deterrence threat holds at risk what the adversary values and what an American president would be willing to do in defense of those U.S. and allied interests. U.S. counterforce targeting is likely a more credible and thus effective basis for deterrence, and also potentially able to meet the principles of the JWD, even though it requires a larger, dynamic nuclear force; a policy of intentionally targeting societies likely is less credible and expressly violates the JWD principles of discrimination and proportionality, even if it requires fewer nuclear weapons. When advocating a countervalue strategy and reducing U.S. nuclear weapons, proponents typically downplay or ignore the potential differences in loss of innocent life—countervalue targeting could lead to tens of millions more innocent lives lost.

Schlesinger was echoing the analysis of the 1960's futurist Herman Kahn, who reasoned that humility requires the strategist to admit that deterrence is not necessarily predictably successful and that it would be wise to prepare for the possibility that deterrence might fail. Kahn wrote:

> Once one accepts the idea that deterrence is not absolutely reliable and that it would be possible to survive a war, then he may be willing to buy insurance—to spend money on preparations to decrease the number of fatalities and injuries, limit damage, facilitate recuperation, and to get the best

---

[195] Ibid., p. 129.

military result possible—at least "to prevail" in
some meaningful sense if you cannot win.[196]

Thus, Muskie, while focusing on the warfighting
potential of weapons, was missing the larger point that it
was the credibility of the warfighting potential that
bolstered the primary object of the force: to deter the
adversary from initiating war in the first place.

If the United States was to earnestly seek to deter
adversaries from employing nuclear weapons, and lessen
the coercive impact of their nuclear weapons, the Jimmy
Carter Administration assessed that the United States was
wise to develop a nuclear deterrence strategy that
effectively convinced the Soviets that nuclear war should
not be dared and therefore to choose peace over aggression.

After significant debate among defense planners, in July
1980, Democratic President Jimmy Carter signed
Presidential Directive-59 (PD-59) which embraced and
extended this deterrence paradigm introduced during the
Republican Nixon Administration by Secretary
Schlesinger.[197] Carter's PD-59 aimed at providing the
President of the United States more options to respond to a
variety of possible Soviet threats and attacks. Carter, like his
predecessor, added counterforce targeting options to hold
at risk the adversary's weapons and instruments of regime
power and control. PD-59 stated that "To continue to deter
in an era of strategic nuclear equivalence, it is necessary to

---

[196] Herman Kahn, *On Thermonuclear War*, op. cit., p. 24.

[197] President Jimmy Carter, *Presidential Directive/NSC-59* (Washington,
D.C.: The White House, July 25, 1980), available at
https://nsarchive2.gwu.edu/nukevault/ebb390/docs/7-25-
80%20PD%2059.pdf. For further information on the chronology of
events related to PD-59, including evidence that President Carter made
the decision to sign PD-59 prior to its contents being briefed to Secretary
of State Muskie, see Zbigniew Brzezinski *Chronology of PD-59
Memorandum* (White House), available at
https://nsarchive2.gwu.edu/nukevault/ebb390/docs/8-22-
80%20Brz%20chron.pdf.

have nuclear (as well as conventional) forces such that in considering aggression against our interests an adversary would recognize that no plausible outcome would represent a victory on any plausible definition of victory." It went on to outline the strategy for meeting those deterrence requirements.

> To this end and so as to preserve the possibility of bargaining effectively to terminate the war on acceptable terms that are as favorable as practical, if deterrence fails initially, we must be capable of fighting successfully so that the adversary would not achieve his war aims and would suffer costs that are unacceptable, or in any event greater than his gains, from having initiated attack.[198]

The Single Integrated Operational Plan (SIOP), according to the PD-59, would provide targeting options against the Soviet Union and its allies, considering a variety of contingencies. The targeting plans would be characterized by flexibility and would also rely on reserve forces that could bolster and help execute the Carter countervailing strategy. Furthermore, PD-59 went on to outline the categories of the possible targets. These targets would be characterized by the high value that the adversary regime placed on them. These targets would include strategic and theater nuclear weapons and storage; military command, control, communications, and intelligence capabilities (C3I); all other military forces including stationary and mobile; and industrial facilities that would sustain the war effort.[199] This approach to deterrence, holding at risk what the United States assessed the Soviets valued most, was key to understanding the adaptations in

---

[198] Carter, *Presidential Directive/NSC-59*, op. cit., p. 1.

[199] Ibid., p. 3.

both NSDM-242 and PD-59.[200] The approach considered the capabilities and the doctrines of the adversary and, according to National Security Adviser Zbigniew Brzezinski, is "thus more likely to deter him effectively."[201] PD 59's determinations were firmly based on the December 13, 1978, nuclear targeting policy review directed by Leon Sloss.[202] This decisive report would be known simply as the "Sloss Report."

At the time, the Carter policy, just as Nixon's, was criticized by some in the public and Congress. The focus on flexibility and targeting the adversary's means of warfighting led some to assert that the Carter Administration was preparing for nuclear war and thereby tempting nuclear warfighting.[203] The preferred alternative to the flexible and discriminate targeting, was a force that had fewer options and that focused on targeting cities. Strictly from a military planning perspective, having fewer nuclear response options that could not hold at risk what the adversary valued—that is, the adversary regime's ability to survive, to maintain regime control, and to carry out its military objectives—risked having a nuclear force

---

[200] See, for example Edward C. Keefer, *Harold Brown : Offsetting the Soviet military challenge 1977–1981* (Washington, D.C.: Government Printing Office, 2017), p. 149, available at https://history.defense.gov/Portals/70/Documents/secretaryofdefense/OSDSeries_Vol9.pdf.

[201] Ibid., p. 144, quoting from memoirs of Zbigniew Brzezinski, Power and Principle: Memoirs of the National Security Adviser, 1977–1981 (New York, NY: Farrar Straus Giroux, 1983), p. 459.

[202] Memorandum from Leon Sloss, Director, Nuclear Targeting Policy Review, for the Joint Staff of the Department of Defense, originally Top Secret, declassified 2013, available at https://www.archives.gov/files/declassification/iscap/pdf/2011-002-doc1.pdf.

[203] Richard Burt, "Carter Shifts U.S. Strategy for Deterring Nuclear War," *The New York Times*, February 10, 1979, https://www.nytimes.com/1979/02/10/archives/carter-shifts-us-strategy-for-deterring-nuclear-war-debate-foreseen.html.

that left the United States with inadequate options to retaliate against the adversary in a variety of contingencies and in ways the adversary would believe. In other words, the critics of NSDM-242 and PD-59 favored an alternative approach to deterrence that basically was a return to McNamara's "Assured Destruction" quotients and would likely be less credible for preventing war.

The changes in U.S. deterrence policy found in NSDM-242 and PD-59 were based on the bipartisan conclusion that McNamara's earlier approach to deterrence would undermine the credibility of deterrence in the minds of U.S. adversaries and therefore create an unacceptable degree of risk that deterrence would fail. Furthermore, if deterrence did fail, and the United States had eschewed a countervailing strategy, the United States would have few, if any, credible limited options to retaliate against the adversary in a way to communicate to him that he would not prevail by continued attacks and that the United States had a variety of responses for any eventuality that he may be planning. A larger, flexible, well-hedged force not only would equip the United States with a spectrum of response options to achieve its military aims but also enable the United States to signal to the adversary that the United States can make the war go even worse for him, and thereby bargain with him to steer the adversary to end the war at the lowest levels of violence and destruction possible.

Those who criticized NSDM-242 and PD-59 as so-called nuclear "warfighting" strategies were arguing against the policies and planning that made actual nuclear warfighting less likely. The uncomfortable reality is that the critics' inflexible force concept—with smaller numbers of systems and weapons that intentionally targeted cities—was more dangerous and tempted deterrence failure that would cripple U.S. response options and more likely lead to widespread societal destruction.

President Ronald Reagan embraced and extended the Nixon and Carter paradigms for deterrence as a means of increasing its credibility and effectiveness.

The 1981 National Security Decision Directive 13 (NSDD-13) laid out the Reagan nuclear employment policy for the purposes of strengthening the credibility of U.S. deterrence against the Soviets. NSDD-13 stated:

> Deterrence can best be achieved if our defense posture makes Soviet assessments of war outcomes, under any contingency, so uncertain and dangerous as to remove any incentive for initiating attack. This requires that we be convincingly capable of responding in such a way that the Soviets or other adversary would be denied their political and military objectives. Stated otherwise, we must be prepared to wage war successfully. [204]

And, like the Carter Administration's policy, it also planned for a variety of contingencies if deterrence initially failed. It stated:

> The United States must be able to deny the Soviet Union a military victory at any level of conflict and force it to seek earliest termination of hostilities on terms favorable to United States. To this end, we must have your capability to attack the widest range of targets in a way that serves our national interests, even when retaliating to a massive strike, received without strategic warning, and if necessary to cripple the capability of the Soviet Union and its allies to conduct effective military operations.[205]

---

[204] Ibid., p.1.

[205] Reagan, *National Security Decision Directive Number 13*, op. cit.

It went on to expressly direct that the targeting not only avoid cities but also seek to limit collateral damage in possible attacks against legitimate military targets. And, to better protect the American people and to bolster the strength of U.S. efforts to credibly deter the Soviets, the Reagan Administration famously argued that there is a significant role for active missile defenses to reduce "the likelihood of coercion and increased prospects for postwar recovery of the United States."[206] Reagan initiated the plan to deploy missile defenses in space called the Strategic Defense Initiative (SDI) and made explicitly moral arguments for doing so.[207] He even went so far as offering the possibility of sharing the defensive technology with other nations including the Soviets.[208]

This was one of Reagan's greatest contributions to statecraft and strategic thought: not only was it immoral to target cities as such, but Reagan also argued it was immoral to intentionally permit American cities to remain vulnerable when the country had the ability as a nation to better protect them. It also risked deterrence failure; indeed, it would be more convincing to adversaries that the United States would engage in strategic strikes if the adversary knew the United States could defend its country if the aggressor retaliated. To strengthen the credibility of U.S. deterrence, the United States should not only seek to advance its offensive forces, but also invest in the technologies to blunt

---

[206] President Ronald Reagan, *National Security Decision Directive Number 13* (Washington, D.C.: The White House, October 19, 1981), p. 4, available at https://irp.fas.org/offdocs/nsdd/nsdd-13.pdf.

[207] See President Ronald Reagan, Address To the Nation on Defense and National Security, March 23, 1983, available at https://www.reaganlibrary.gov/archives/speech/address-nation-defense-and-national-security.

[208] Excerpts from President Ronald Reagan Interview with British Broadcasters, *The New York Times*, October 31, 1985, Section A, Page 12, available at EXCERPTS FROM REAGAN INTERVIEW WITH BRITISH BROADCASTERS - The New York Times (nytimes.com).

a Soviet attack and shield the American people. To Reagan, morality and credible deterrence against the Soviets were reinforcing.

Around the same time, strategists Colin Gray and Keith Payne articulated additional benefits of missile defense including to dissuade the adversary from believing that the United States would be deterred from defending its vital interests by possibly employing a nuclear weapon first, and by protecting deterrence options during a protracted conflict wherein the United States would persist in trying to control escalation.[209] Importantly, while Reagan argued in his speeches for an aspirational aim of replacing threats of nuclear retaliation with robust and global missile defenses, he did not lessen the U.S. investment or commitment to nuclear deterrence. Indeed, building on the earlier initiative of Carter as part of the "Countervailing Strategy," Reagan upgraded all three legs of the nuclear triad, initiated the development of the MX missile, the B-1 Lancer and what would become the B-2 bomber. He also directed the replacement of the older ballistic missiles with the advanced D-5 sea-launched ballistic missile on the U.S. Trident submarines.[210] It wasn't just that he directed cutting-edge strategic nuclear modernization; at the request of European allies, Reagan also sent 108 highly-accurate Pershing II ballistic missiles to West Germany and 256 of planned 464 ground-launched cruise missiles (GLCMs) called "Gryphons" to West Germany and the United Kingdom, Belgium, and Italy.[211] Still, critics accused the Reagan

---

[209] See, Matthew R. Costlow, *Restraints at the Nuclear Brink, Factors in Keeping War Limited, Occasional Paper*, Vol. 2, No. 7. (Fairfax, VA: National Institute Press, July 2023), p. 12, available at https://nipp.org/wp-content/uploads/2023/07/OP-Vol.-3-No.-7.pdf.

[210] William Inboden, *The Peacemaker: Ronald Reagan, the Cold War, and the World on the Brink* (Dutton, 2022) pp. 108-109. When the INF Treaty was signed, 208 GLCMs remained to be deployed, including in the Netherlands.

[211] Ibid., p. 256.

Administration, as they had criticized the earlier Nixon and Carter Administrations, of making nuclear war more likely by adapting and expanding U.S. nuclear forces to bolster the credibility of U.S. nuclear deterrence.

Albert Wohlstetter admonished those who would use JWD arguments to oppose improving or adapting nuclear forces to increase confidence in deterrence. He said, "Many believe that MAD has kept the nuclear peace and is therefore necessary, at least as myth. But the evolution of doctrines and polices of deterrence [away from MAD] needs to be seen in relation to the changing technologies of discrimination and control as well as the technologies of nuclear brute force."[212] As technology improved, and as strategists sought to improve U.S. options to credibly deter adversaries, the United States was only right to integrate those technologies and weapons systems to continually seek to limit collateral damage to the adversary and societal damage to the United States while optimizing the credibility of deterrence. That was all to support the goal of deterring adversaries who were threatening aggression in service of their national aims, which threatened the peace, security, and freedom of Americans and allies.

Another example of adapting strategic deterrence as the threats changed and technology developed was President George W. Bush's decision to withdraw the United States from the 1972 Anti-Ballistic Missile (ABM) Treaty on December 13, 2001. Explaining his decision, Bush said:

> We know that the terrorists, and some of those who support them seek the ability to deliver death and destruction to our doorstep via missile. And we must have the freedom and the flexibility to develop effective defenses against those attacks. Defending the American people is my highest

---

[212] Wohlstetter, "Bishops, Statemen, and Other Strategists on the Bombing of Innocents," op. cit., p. 19.

priority as Commander in Chief, and I cannot and will not allow the United States to remain in a treaty that prevents us from developing effective defenses.[213]

The homeland missile defense system under George W. Bush would be designed to defend the homeland against terrorist and rogue regimes that some experts surmised might not be deterrable, and not missile attacks from peer states like Russia; Bush said that the relationship between the United States and Russia at the time was moving in a constructive direction and did not require strategic missile defense.

President Barack Obama also directed his Pentagon to add to homeland defense when the rogue state missile threat from North Korea grew more acute, and conditioned further development of defenses if the threat from rogue nation Iran also continued.[214] Missile defense's role has continued to evolve, along with its technology. For example, the Trump Administration's 2019 *Missile Defense Review* noted that missile defense should be expanded in response to new threats against allies and the homeland. It stated:

> Missile defense contributes directly to tailored U.S. deterrence strategies for regional missile threats and for rogue state ICBM threats to the U.S. homeland. Missile defenses can undermine potential adversaries' confidence in their ability to achieve their intended political or military

---

[213] President George W. Bush, "President Discusses National Missile Defense," *Whitehouse.gov*, December 13, 2001, available at https://georgewbush-whitehouse.archives.gov/news/releases/2001/12/20011213-4.html.

[214] Phil Steward and David Alexander, "US to bolster missile defenses to counter North Korea threat," *Reuters*, March 15, 2013, available at https://www.reuters.com/article/korea-north-usa-defense-idINDEE92E0D720130315.

objectives through missile threats or attacks. An adversary's uncertainty regarding the effectiveness of its attack plans, combined with the prospect of an effective U.S. response to aggression, provide strong incentives for adversary restraint if ever contemplating missile attacks. By shaping an adversary's decision calculus in this way, missile defense diminishes the perceived value of missiles as tools of coercion and aggression, thus contributing to deterrence.[215]

Even as recently as the Biden Administration's 2022 Missile Defense Review, the official U.S. policy is to continue to improve homeland missile defense against the threats from North Korea and possibly Iran, but not against the strategic threats Russia or the PRC can present.[216] The nation currently remains vulnerable to the nuclear peer nation threats, including even coercive limited strikes. Closing this vulnerability by pursuing and deploying as soon as possible defenses against potential coercive strikes by China or Russia would offer protection of innocent Americans who are currently vulnerable to peer adversary attack. It would also bolstering deterrence by causing adversaries to doubt the likelihood of the success of those strikes.[217]

---

[215] U.S. Department of Defense, *2019 Missile Defense Review* (Washington, D.C.: Department of Defense, 2018), p. VII, available at https://media.defense.gov/2019/Jan/17/2002080666/-1/-1/1/2019-MISSILE-DEFENSE-REVIEW.PDF.

[216] U.S. Department of Defense, *2022 Missile Defense Review* (Washington, D.C.: Department of Defense, 2022), p. 1, available at https://media.defense.gov/2022/Oct/27/2003103845/-1/-1/1/2022-NATIONAL-DEFENSE-STRATEGY-NPR-MDR.PDF.

[217] See Rebeccah L. Heinrichs and John E. Hyten, "The U.S. Must Upgrade its Missile Defence to Deter Russia and China," Royal United Services Institute, April 2, 2024, available at The US Must Upgrade its Missile Defence to Deter Russia and China | Royal United Services Institute (rusi.org).

Obama, while perhaps most famous for his desire to lead the world down a path to zero nuclear weapons and earning a Nobel Peace Prize for this aspiration, ultimately agreed with the bipartisan Congressional view to continue significant investments in the modernization of the nuclear weapons enterprise and its associated delivery systems.[218] And, while negotiating further nuclear weapons reductions with the Russian Federation, Obama also embraced the decades-long bipartisan consensus that is the basis for American strategic deterrence policy: to continue having counterforce targeting capabilities and *not* targeting civilians intentionally. The unclassified guidance says:

> The new guidance requires the United States to maintain significant counterforce capabilities against potential adversaries. The new guidance does not rely on a "counter value," or "minimum deterrence" strategy. The new guidance makes clear that all plans must be consistent with the fundamental principles of the Law of Armed Conflict. Accordingly, plans will, for example, apply the principles of distinction and proportionality, and seek to minimize collateral damage to civilian populations and civilian objects. The United States will not intentionally target civilian populations or civilian objects.[219]

To be clear, while Obama famously sought a "world without nuclear weapons" he did not abandon the fundamental mission of nuclear deterrence nor the U.S.

---

[218] Philip Ewing, "Obama's Nuclear Paradox: Pushing for Cuts, Agreeing to Upgrades," *National Public Radio*, May 25, 2016, available at https://www.npr.org/sections/parallels/2016/05/25/479498018/oba mas-nuclear-paradox-pushing-for-cuts-agreeing-to-upgrades.

[219] U.S. Department of Defense, *2013 Report to Congress on the Nuclear Employment Strategy of the United States* (specified in Section 491 of 10 U.S.C., delivered June 2013), pp. 4-5, available at https://apps.dtic.mil/sti/pdfs/ADA590745.pdf.

approach to deterrence that had developed since the 1970s. Obama also initiated, even if far more slowly and haltingly, a nuclear modernization program, and embraced the nuclear triad of delivery systems. Further, U.S. nuclear weapons would provide the ultimate security for U.S. and allies 'vital interests; the posture and kind of nuclear weapons would be developed based on then-current security requirements. The Obama Administration's sincere desire to eliminate nuclear weapons, it did not eschew the basic tenets of U.S. deterrence strategy. Across administrations, the fundamental principles of nuclear deterrence have held. Keith Payne and David Trachtenberg emphasized, "For over five decades and on a fully bipartisan basis, the United States has explicitly rejected a 'counter-city,' 'minimum deterrence' policy—sometimes also referred to as an 'assured destruction' threat—despite its relatively modest retaliatory force requirements, because of its potential incredibility as a deterrent and its moral repugnance."[220]

Over the years, there have been persistent objections to bipartisan U.S. efforts to increase the credibility of deterrence over claims that to increase its credibility is preparing for a limited nuclear war and thereby increasing the likelihood of nuclear employment. Schlesinger's response from decades ago are instruction. But there is no evidence that preparing for the possibility of limited nuclear employment to prevent an adversary from prevailing using nuclear weapons make nuclear war-fighting more likely. Indeed, the expressed purpose of planning for limited nuclear employment is to deter the adversary's initial act of nuclear or non-nuclear aggression that could lead to

---

[220] Keith B. Payne and David J. Trachtenberg, *Deterrence in the Emerging Threat Environment: What is Different and Why it Matters, Occasional Paper*, Vol. 2, No. 8 (Fairfax, VA: National Institute Press, August 2022), p. 39, available at https://nipp.org/wp-content/uploads/2022/08/OP-Vol.-2-No.-8.pdf.

strategic attacks and the destruction of U.S. and allied core interests. O'Brien counters that the U.S. military leaders most familiar with nuclear weapons tend to be quite conservative in contemplating options for acceptable use, rather than eager for it.[221]

Payne and Coleman, writing in 1988 when Reagan was expanding the U.S. nuclear force to deter the Soviets and encourage diplomacy to end the Cold War with a just peace, point out that U.S. limited nuclear options had become central to U.S. strategic targeting and deterrence policy. They wrote that the value of flexible options for deterrence, preparations for limited nuclear employment, and the need to discriminate between military and societal targets, all were recognized by some U.S. officials in the 1960s.[222] They outline how U.S. nuclear deterrence planning was refined until reaching the consensus deterrence strategy that the United States continues to embrace today. As noted above, in 1974, Nixon's Secretary of Defense James Schlesinger made it official U.S. policy to seek flexible, accurate forces to help the United States establish credible strategic deterrence and extended deterrence for allies in varying circumstances.   Carter's official planning documents embraced these views as well. And, the Reagan Administration's Secretary of Defense, Caspar Weinberger, maintained that continuity and made it publicly explicit that U.S. policy is to minimize civilian casualties and to not intentionally target populations.[223]

It is hardly compelling to insist that preparing for moral, nuclear employment if deterrence fails for the express purpose of bolstering deterrence will necessarily lead to nuclear employment when the evidence of four decades of nuclear peace and the avoidances of major power war

---

[221] William V. O'Brien and John P. Langan, *The Nuclear Dilemma and the Just War Tradition* (Lexington, MA: Lexington Books, April 1986), p.174.

[222] Keith B. Payne and Jill E. Coleman, op. cit., p. 79.

[223] See Ibid., p. 79 for a discussion of this change in thinking.

shows that this has not been the case. Although William Perry and Tom Collina argued for nuclear disarmament in their book *The Button: The New Nuclear Arms Race and Presidential Power from Truman to Trump,* the authors' observation about the evidence supporting nuclear restraint was welcome and instructive. They wrote, "Clearly, there is a strong reluctance among U.S. presidents to pull the nuclear trigger, as evidenced by the fact that the bomb has not been used in an attack since 1945 and was not used in the face of military stalemates, like Korea, or defeats, like Vietnam."[224]

Those who employ the JWD in favor of nuclear disarmament have not succeeded in persuading American administrations, or any other nuclear-armed state to adopt their views in practice. Since the 1970s, even when presidents publicly held out the goal of global nuclear disarmament, their official documents and deterrence strategies remained consistent in the most basic ways. What did change was the evolution of U.S. policy to adopt flexible, counterforce targeting to hold at risk what the adversary values most, and to intentionally seek to minimize civilian death and societal destruction. At the same time, as strategists sought to increase the credibility of U.S. deterrence options in this way, Pentagon officials also made explicit the aim to limit civilian harm that complemented the approach. Reagan's Secretary of Defense Caspar Weinberger was one of the most emphatic apologists of this clarified policy. He said the United States "...consciously does not target population and, in fact, has provisions for reducing civilian casualties."[225] Indeed, Henry Kissinger, perhaps one of the most famous realist

---

[224] William Perry and Tom Collina, *The Button: The New Nuclear Arms Race and Presidential Power from Truman to Trump* (Dallas, TX: BenBella Books, 2020), p. 102.

[225] Caspar Weinberger, "U.S. Defense Strategy," *Foreign Affairs*, Vol. 64, No. 4 (Spring 1986), pp. 680-681.

practitioners in the prime of his career, shared Weinberger's view of the morality of only targeting military objects and believed that intentionally targeting of societal targets is "the height of immorality."[226]

Targeting cities would violate the JWD principle of discrimination and likely undermine deterrence, which would increase the risk of far worse injustice and innocent loss of life and liberty. While the United States could not possibly know with certainty if nuclear exchanges could be kept limited and would not lead to the highest levels of escalation and violence, opting to not even try would likely undermine deterrence and make the most destructive outcome in war more likely. Failing to prepare for the variety of eventualities to minimize the destruction and convince the enemy to end the war on the lowest levels of violence would be an abrogation of the U.S. Constitution's requirement to provide for the common defense as well as the Divine duty of government to protect the innocent and thwart those who seek their destruction.

The JWD and efforts to improve the credibility of U.S. deterrence options have been reinforcing and are not in conflict. As the United States has sought to increase the credibility of its nuclear deterrence options and added complementary defensive options within its strategic deterrence strategy, it has increasingly embraced the same principles of the JWD evident in other U.S. military documents that shape and guide deterrence and warfare. This development was not coincidental; Secretary Weinberger said in a then-classified memo to the Chairman

---

[226] Henry Kissinger quote appears in the minutes of a Verification Panel Meeting in the White House Situation Room in August 1973. For additional information, declassified access is available in the Department of State, Foreign Relations of the United States, 1969-1976, Vol. XXXV, National Security Policy, 1973-1976 (Washington, D.C.: U.S. Government Printing Office, 2014), p. 105, available at https://static.history.state.gov/frus/frus1969-76v35/pdf/frus1969-76v35.pdf#page=147.

of the JCS that intentionally targeting civilians was to be avoided because he deemed it to be inconsistent with "Western morality."[227]

In his famous article in Foreign Affairs, Weinberger explained quite plainly, "We do not, in fact, plan our retaliatory options to maximize Soviet casualties or to attack deliberately the Soviet population. Indeed, we believe such a doctrine would be neither moral nor prudent." In the following lines where Weinberger would explain why the United States did not conduct nuclear targeting for the purposes of deterring the Soviets by hoping to maximize civilian deaths, one can see logical appeals to the principles of discrimination and proportionality tied directly to what would credibly convince the adversary to act with restraint by holding at risk what he values, not necessarily what Americans would value most. He said, "It is not moral because the Soviet people should not deliberately be made the victims of any U.S. retaliation to an attack launched by the Soviet leadership—a leadership for which the Soviet people are not responsible and cannot control. It is not prudent because secure deterrence should be based on the threat to destroy what the Soviet leadership values most highly: namely, itself, its military power and political control capabilities, and its industrial ability to wage war." In this clear articulation, Weinberger comes close to summarizing the remarkable transformation of the U.S. nuclear deterrence policy, forged successfully at the height of the Cold War when Americans were under enormous strain to deter a peer nuclear adversary, something they had never been forced to do in the years immediately following the Second World War. Weinberger took on directly those

---

[227] Quoted in Keith B. Payne, *The Rejection of Intentional Population Targeting for "Tripolar" Deterrence, Occasional Paper*, Vol. 3, No. 9, (Fairfax, VA: National Institute Press, September 2023), p. 29, available at https://nipp.org/papers/the-rejection-of-intentional-population-targeting-for-tripolar-deterrence/.

critics who believed the moral high ground belonged to the nuclear disarmers and that the world was closer to the brink of nuclear war due to Reagan's build-up. Weinberger responded, "No one who has received as many briefings on nuclear weapons or participated in crisis exercises as I have could hold any doubts about the absolute necessity of avoiding nuclear war. It is precisely because of this necessity that the United States must have a secure deterrent. Moreover, developing selective, discriminate responses is manifestly moral." The peace that so many desired then and clearly desire now should not cost American policymakers an act or even a plan to act grossly immoral. But they did not have to. Indeed, morality, that is—justice, and peace, could go hand in glove, even at the most stressing point thus far in the Nuclear Age.

The reality that the JWD is compatible with and has even reinforced improvements in the credibility of U.S. nuclear deterrence since the 1960s is the fundamental finding of this project. During this time, Republican and Democratic administrations have embraced the same tenets of nuclear deterrence: to hold at risk what the enemy values (which for authoritarians are not their civilians) and to spare innocent life to the extent possible. While the United States waged deterrence in this manner, the nuclear peace has held. It would be wise to maintain this approach, and to adapt the nuclear posture to credibly deter the changing threats while seeking to comply with the JWD. Forgoing the goal of complying with the LOAC as the United States seeks to bolster the credibility of deterrence against China, Russia, and others would risk not only abandoning the principles that give the United States moral clarity but also the grave possibility of deterrence failure.

Conclusion

The nuclear threats to the United States are numerous and dynamic and have grown since the Cold War. The United States now faces two determined and increasingly aggressive peer nuclear adversaries. This is unprecedented. Despite the idealist aspiration to transform the international system so that a benevolent global government like the United Nations can arbitrate conflict between nations and facilitate nuclear disarmament, the world is no closer to achieving that vision than at the close of the Second World War. Without having the luxury of waiting for a miraculous global transformation, American statesmen and strategists have sought to strengthen U.S. security and the protection of the American people and its allies.

In the wake of the Second World War, U.S. administrations developed and then improved upon and made explicit paradigms to calibrate forces and policies that would optimize the success of U.S. deterrence. Through the 1960s, U.S. nuclear deterrence did include the expressed targeting of civilians for deterrent effect. But strategy evolved and the thinking became more refined at the start of the next decade and phase of the Cold War.

The Schlesinger Doctrine, established upon NSSM-169, not only sought to refine U.S. strategy to strengthen the credibility of U.S. deterrence in the minds of the Soviets, but also began the process of bringing U.S. deterrence policy more in line with the principles of the JWD. President Carter embraced Nixon's approach and cemented the bipartisan nature of what every Democrat and Republican presidency has since affirmed, even if each altered and adapted various aspects of the strategic posture, whether by building on missile defense, by adding supplemental delivery systems, or by eliminating certain weapon systems such as the Titan

II ICBMs, which had the highest yield nuclear warheads on an ICBM, and relatively poor accuracy.[228]

Subsequent administrations have rejected intentional targeting of civilian populations as a violation of the LOAC, and embraced nuclear postures that would provide some active defenses and flexible response options to hold at risk what adversaries value most. The object of flexible response options (and defenses to maximize the survival of U.S. options) for a variety of possible contingencies is to create an incentive for a potential adversary to choose restraint and de-escalation and war resolution rather than further escalation and violence. For example, the Trump Administration's *2020 Nuclear Employment Strategy of the United States*, states, "[T]he U.S. nuclear planning and targeting adhere to the laws of armed conflict. The United States has for decades rejected a deterrence strategy based on purposely threatening civilian populations, and the United States will not intentionally target civilian populations." [229] The Biden Administration's 2022 *Nuclear Posture Review* likewise states: "Longstanding DoD policy is to comply with LOAC in armed conflict however characterized, and the DoD Law of War Manual recognizes that '[t]he law of war governs the use of nuclear weapons, just as it governs the use of conventional weapons.' In addition, longstanding U.S. policy is to not purposely threaten civilian populations or objects, and the United States will not intentionally target civilian populations or objects in violation of the LOAC."[230]

---

[228] For additional information on the history of the Titan Missile program, including the specifications of the Titan II, see Titan Missile Museum, available at https://titanmissilemuseum.org/about/titan-ii-history/.

[229] See U.S. Department of Defense, *2020 Report to Congress on the Nuclear Employment Strategy of the United States*, op. cit.

[230] U.S. Department of Defense, *Nuclear Posture Review* 2022, op. cit.

Some prominent religious organizations and secular anti-nuclear groups have protested U.S. government efforts to improve the credibility of deterrence. And yet, those with the duty to protect the nation and is people and who are in positions of authority, when faced with the reality of the dangers threatening the country, have not broken from the established and successful strategy of deterrence. U.S. strategy has sought to strengthen the credibility of deterrence by focusing on military and regime objects and by avoiding targeting civilians and societal targets intentionally.

Deterrence strategy has also maintained flexibility to plan for a variety of contingencies if deterrence fails and thereby to optimize the U.S. ability to retaliate in limited ways that would steer adversaries away from escalation and towards peace on terms that would help to protect the United States and allies. These limited options are key to reinforcing the deterrence of aggression in the first place. The adversary's belief in the possibility and even plausibility of this outcome, then, helps convince him to decide not to go down the path of aggression — it deters him. In each of these instances, the U.S. has moved towards bolstering the credibility of deterrence and reinforced the principles of protecting the innocent with the aim of a just and lasting peace.

This study concludes that as U.S. professional strategists sought to credibly deter, they also moved increasingly toward adherence to JWD principles. Credibly deterring U.S. adversaries and adhering to JWD have not been in conflict; instead, they have been reinforcing. Failing to maintain credible deterrence in favor of disarmament objectives, and clinging to notions of MAD, at a time when the risk of deterrence failure appears to be rising, would unacceptably raise the risk that deterrence will fail — allowing only options that unnecessarily increase death and destruction, provide no defense of innocents at home, and portend catastrophic consequences such as the victory of authoritarians and the squelching of American liberty.

Nuclear strategists have had to concede in humility that there is great uncertainty about how nuclear escalation may unfold if deterrence fails. But that uncertainty does not obviate the government's duty to limit the potential destruction to the extent possible, defend the innocent, and preserve a just peace. As Niebuhr concluded, "[T]the notion that the excessive violence of atomic warfare has ended the possibility of a just war does not stand up. The moral problem has been altered, but not eliminated."[231] The United States has a moral duty and Constitutional requirement to maintain credible deterrence options and the JWD provides guidelines for the U.S. strategist and policymaker as he further adapts deterrence options to credibly meet the modern threats.

The reality of living in an anarchic and often violent world among adversaries in possession or pursuit of nuclear weapons makes the demand even greater for governments to prepare to deter adversaries credibly. The JWD is an amalgam of principles and thought predicated on the embrace of a realist international relations framework. Trying to fit the JWD into the Atomic Age while holding presuppositions that are unique to an idealist framework for international relations will lead to incoherent and outright logical contradictions.

The heart of successful deterrence is to convince adversaries that plausible strategic attacks against the United States or allies will not be worth the cost. A strategic attack may elicit a U.S. response that will prevent the aggressor from prevailing and will exact an unacceptable cost such that the adversary will conclude that the initial act of aggression is not worth the cost. To be a just and

---

[231] Henry R. Davis and Robert C. Good, *Reinhold Niebuhr On Politics: His Political Philosophy and Its Application to Our Age as Expressed in His Writings* (Eugene, OR: Wipf and Stock Publishers, 1960) p. 145.

righteous government and government servant, it is not enough to simply desire peace and to possess sincere intent to foster peace and avoid harm and violence. The just government and just war strategist must be devoted to affecting events that will result in the peace and justice they so sincerely intend. The JWD principles, including and especially the principle of proportionality during a just war, cannot be evaluated or acted upon without carefully weighing the value of what the just warrior is defending and from what he is defending against.

The just war strategist must engage with doctrinal principles, recognizing there are actions that are inherently wrong, while *of course* weighing potential consequences of certain actions or inaction and pursuing the greatest possible good (as defined by maximizing the protection of the innocent and punishing those trying to harm them).[232]

To bolster the credibility of deterrence in the current context—the early stages of a Cold War with the PRC and Russia and a possible Sino-Russian entente—the United States should maintain the time-tested paradigm of deterrence. Strategists should prepare to deter both countries simultaneously. The bi-partisan Congressionally mandated U.S. Strategic Posture Commission stated:

> The United States faces a fundamentally different strategic setting than it has experienced during the past 70 years. Indeed, the Commission perceives the coming years as a "decisive decade" during which the United States must simultaneously deter two nuclear-armed adversaries and assure its many concerned Allies, all while undertaking a significant modernization of its conventional and nuclear capabilities. Given these stakes, the challenge is to build a strategic posture that has the

---

[232] Lubomir Martin Ondrasek, "Jean Bethke Elshtain: An Augustinian at War," *Providence Magazine*, August 11, 2017.

highest probability to secure and further U.S. vital interests into the future as well as prevent a major power war or nuclear employment of any kind.[233]

To bolster the credibility of deterrence against both nations, the United States should be equipped with the weapons to hold at risk the targets that both adversary regimes value, and adequately postured to employ in a variety of contingencies, in ways that minimize the risk to the defender if deterrence fails. And the United States should bolster U.S. active missile defenses to defend its most critical assets, allies, and the American people.[234] As the United States attempts to achieve its military objectives at the lowest levels of violence necessary, the goal should be to convince its adversary to stand down rather than escalate further. The United States should also continue to affirm the LOAC and comply with it in its deterrence policy and targeting strategy. This means the United States should prepare to limit the damage of an aggressor's attack, steer the adversary towards a conclusion of the war on terms most favorable to the United States, and avoid the intentional targeting of innocents. Keeping nations as far away as possible from the precipice of nuclear employment requires improving the credibility of deterrence to maximize the chances of convincing authoritarian countries that it is in their interests to avoid war with the United States. And if America's enemies choose war and deterrence

---

[233] Congressional Commission on the Strategic Posture of the United States, October 2023, op. cit., p. 5.

[234] Adapting missile defense to defend against the coercive threat from China and Russia was also one of the findings of the Congressional Commission on the Strategic Posture of the United States 2023, op. cit., p. x. Please also see John Hyten and Rebeccah L. Heinrichs, "The U.S. Much Upgrade its Missile Defense to Deter Russia and China," *Royal United Services Institute*, April 2, 2024, available at https://www.rusi.org/explore-our-research/publications/commentary/us-must-upgrade-its-missile-defence-deter-russia-and-china.

fails, the United States must be prepared to prevail, to protect innocents, and to preserve the American way of life. This preparation strengthens deterrence. And especially today, when the stakes are so high, credibly deterring nuclear adversaries is the most important and moral duty of the American policymaker.

About the Author

Rebeccah L. Heinrichs is a Senior Fellow at Hudson Institute and the Director of its Keystone Defense Initiative. She specializes in national defense and foreign policy.

Dr. Heinrichs served as a commissioner on the Congressionally mandated 2023 bipartisan Strategic Posture Commission. In May 2024, President Joseph Biden nominated her to be a Republican Commissioner on the bipartisan U.S. Advisory Commission on Public Diplomacy. Dr. Heinrichs also serves on the U.S. Strategic Command Strategic Advisory Group and is co-chair of the Strategic Stability Working Group at the U.S. Institute of Peace. She is a contributing editor to Providence Magazine, a journal dedicated to furthering prudent American statecraft and understanding Christian Realism.

Dr. Heinrichs earned her doctorate in defense and strategic studies from Missouri State University and was honored for outstanding academic achievement. She received her MA in national security and strategic studies from the US Naval War College and graduated with highest distinction from its College of Naval Command and Staff. She earned her BA in history and political science from Ashland University in Ohio, was an Ashbrook Scholar, and currently serves as a member of the Ashbrook board.

Dr. Heinrichs is a longtime member of Capitol Hill Baptist Church, a native of rural Ohio, and resides in Virginia with her husband and their five children.

Index

Commentary on

Duty to Deter
American Nuclear Deterrence and the Just War Doctrine

"To apply timeless insights to present challenges is the highest purpose of scholarship on national security. In *Duty to Deter*, Dr. Rebeccah Heinrichs describes a nuclear deterrence posture consistent with Just War Doctrine that is credible, defensive, flexible—and moral. Americans must relearn this today and should start with this book."

Gary L. Geipel, Ph.D.
Missouri State University
School of Defense and Strategic Studies

"Based on original research and sound analytical reasoning, Rebeccah Heinrichs provides innovative and important insights into the positive interrelationships between nuclear deterrence and just war doctrine. Effectively refuting long held conventional wisdom, this book should be required reading for all theorists and practitioners of deterrence."

Robert G. Joseph, Ph.D.
National Institute for Public Policy

"In this book, Rebeccah Heinrichs confronts the usually ignored question of the morality of the U.S. nuclear based deterrence—the combination of weapons and policy that we rely on to ensure no adversary is ever tempted to attack the United States. She concludes our deterrence meets the moral requirements of the Just War Doctrine."

The Hon. Jon Kyl
former U.S. Senator (AZ)

"In this unflinching moral account of present dangers, Rebeccah Heinrichs enlists just war tradition to equip readers to think with prudence and responsibility about the exercise of American power and the necessity of a robust, moral nuclear policy. Manifesting the tradition's Christian realist grounding, Heinrichs proves herself that rare kind of political thinker: one who insists on responding to the world as it is — not as we would like it to be — while also refusing to jettison moral duties. Delivering hard truths about the moral use of nuclear weapons in preserving order, justice, and peace in the world, *Duty to Deter* is uncomfortable, illuminating, and wise. One does not have to *like* Heinrichs' prescriptions, but we would be fools not to heed them."

Marc LiVecche, Ph.D.
Providence Magazine

"In this compelling book, Rebeccah Heinrichs shows us that the Roman General Vegetius' aphorism that "if you want peace, prepare for war," is more than practical advice. When adversaries possess the most destructive weapons on earth, deterring conflict through strength and preparedness is a moral duty."

Lt. Gen. (ret.) H.R. McMaster, USA
author of Battlegrounds and At War With Ourselves

"There once was a day when moral realism was acknowledged as the foundation of American defense policy, grounded in deep wells of moral reasoning. Today, we are urgently in need of the quality of serious thought and argument represented by Rebecca Heinrichs in *Duty to Deter*. Given the stakes, this book must be welcomed by every serious citizen. It holds the promise of influencing defense policy for good in our increasingly dangerous age."

R. Albert Mohler, Jr., Ph.D.
President and Centennial Professor of Christian Theology
The Southern Baptist Theological Seminary

"Essential reading for a full understanding of an often-overlooked aspect of nuclear and strategic deterrence theory and policy: the moral and legal basis for the U.S. nuclear deterrence posture. Well researched and contains several novel key conclusions that will surprise you."

ADM (ret.) Charles "Chas" Richard, USN
former Commander U.S. Strategic Command

www.ingramcontent.com/pod-product-compliance
Lightning Source LLC
Chambersburg PA
CBHW070832250125
20853CB00021B/387